ROMANS

Grace, Truth, and Redemption

JOHN
MACARTHUR

Table of Contents

ROMANS

Introduction

This epistle's name comes from its original recipients: the members of the church in Rome, the capital of the Roman Empire (1:7).

Author and Date

No one disputes that the apostle Paul wrote Romans. Like his namesake, Israel's first king (Saul was Paul's Hebrew name; Paul his Greek name), Paul was from the tribe of Benjamin (Philippians 3:5). He was also a Roman citizen (Acts 16:37; 22:25). Paul was born about the time of Christ's birth, in Tarsus (Acts 9:11), an important city (Acts 21:39) in the Roman province of Cilicia located in Asia Minor (modern Turkey). He spent much of his early life in Jerusalem as a student of the celebrated rabbi Gamaliel (Acts 22:3). Like his father before him, Paul was a Pharisee (Acts 23:6), a member of the strictest Jewish sect (Philippians 3:5).

Miraculously converted while on his way to Damascus (ca. A.D. 33–34) to arrest Christians in that city, Paul immediately began proclaiming the gospel message (Acts 9:20). After narrowly escaping from Damascus with his life (Acts 9:23–25; 2 Corinthians 11:32–33), Paul spent three years in Nabatean Arabia, south and east of the Dead Sea (Galatians 1:17–18). During that time, he received much of his doctrine as direct revelation from the Lord (Galatians 1:11–12).

More than any other individual, Paul was responsible for the spread of Christianity throughout the Roman Empire. He made three missionary journeys through much of the Mediterranean world, tirelessly preaching the gospel that he had once sought to destroy (Acts 26:9). After Paul returned to Jerusalem bearing an offering for the needy in the church there, he was falsely accused by some Jews

(Acts 21:27–29), savagely beaten by an angry mob (Acts 21:30–31) and arrested by the Romans. Although two Roman governors, Felix and Festus, as well as Herod Agrippa, did not find him guilty of any crime, pressure from the Jewish leaders kept Paul in Roman custody. After two years, the apostle exercised his right as a Roman citizen and appealed his case to Caesar. Through a harrowing trip (Acts 27—28) including a violent, two-week storm at sea that culminated in a shipwreck, Paul reached Rome. Eventually Paul was released for a brief period of ministry, but he was arrested again. Paul suffered martyrdom at Rome in ca. A.D. 65–67 (2 Timothy 4:6).

Though physically unimpressive (2 Corinthians 10:10; Galatians 4:14), Paul possessed an inner strength granted him through the Holy Spirit's power (Philippians 4:13). The grace of God proved sufficient to provide for his every need (2 Corinthians 12:9–10) enabling this noble servant of Christ to success-fully finish his spiritual race (2 Timothy 4:7).

Paul wrote Romans from Corinth, as the references to Phoebe (Romans 16:1, Cenchrea was Corinth's port), Gaius (Romans 16:23), and Erastus (Romans 16:23)—all of whom were associated with Corinth—indicate. The apostle wrote the letter toward the close of his third missionary journey (most likely in A.D. 56), as he prepared to leave for Palestine with an offering for the poor believers in the Jerusalem church (Romans 15:25). Phoebe was given the great responsibility of delivering this letter to the Roman believers (16:1–2).

Background and Setting

Rome was the capital and most important city of the Roman Empire. It was founded in 753 B.C. but is not mentioned in Scripture until New Testament times. Rome is located along the banks of the Tiber River, about fifteen miles from the Mediterranean Sea. Until an artificial harbor was built at nearby Ostia, Rome's main harbor was Puteoli, some hundred and fifty miles away. In Paul's day, the city had a population of over one million people, many of whom were slaves. Rome boasted magnificent buildings, such as the Emperor's palace, the Circus Maximus, and the Forum, but its beauty was marred by the slums in which so many lived. According to tradition Paul was martyred outside Rome on the Ostian Way during Nero's reign (A.D. 54–68).

Some of those converted on the Day of Pentecost probably founded the church at Rome (Acts 2:10). Paul had long sought to visit the Roman church, but had been prevented from doing so (1:13). In God's providence, Paul's inability to visit Rome gave the world this inspired masterpiece of gospel doctrine.

Paul's primary purpose in writing Romans was to teach the great truths of the gospel of grace to believers who had never received apostolic instruction. The letter also introduced him to a church where he was personally unknown but hoped to visit soon for several important reasons: to edify the believers (1:11), to preach the gospel (1:15), and to get to know the Roman Christians so they could encourage him (1:12; 15:32), better pray for him (15:30), and help him with his planned ministry in Spain (15:28).

Unlike with some of Paul's other epistles (for example, 1 Corinthians, 2 Corinthians, and Galatians), his purpose for writing Romans was not to correct aberrant theology or rebuke ungodly living. The Roman church was doctrinally sound, but, like all churches, it was in need of the rich doctrinal and practical instruction this letter provides.

Historical and Theological Themes

Since Romans is primarily a work of doctrine, it contains little historical material. Paul does use such familiar Old Testament figures as Abraham (chapter 4), David (4:6–8), Adam (5:12–21), Sarah (9:9), Rebekah (9:10), Jacob and Esau (9:10–13), and Pharaoh (9:17) as illustrations. He also recounts some of Israel's history (chapters 9—11). Chapter 16 provides insightful glimpses into the nature and character of the first century church and its members.

The overarching theme of Romans is the righteousness that comes from God: the glorious truth that God justifies guilty, condemned sinners by grace alone through faith in Christ alone. Chapters 1—11 present the theological truths of that doctrine, while chapters 12—16 detail its practical outworking in the lives of individual believers and the life of the whole church. Some specific theological topics include principles of spiritual leadership (1:8–15); God's wrath against sinful humankind (1:18–32); principles of divine judgment (2:1–16); the universality of sin (3:9–20); an exposition and defense of justification by faith alone (3:21—4:25); the security of salvation (5:1–11); the transference of Adam's sin (5:12–21); sanctification (chapters 6—8); sovereign election (chapter 9); God's plan for Israel (chapter 11); spiritual gifts and practical godliness (chapter 12); the believer's responsibility to human government (chapter 13); and principles of Christian liberty (14:1—15:12).

Interpretive Challenges

As the preeminent doctrinal work in the New Testament, Romans naturally contains a number of difficult passages. Paul's discussion of the perpetuation of Adam's sin (5:12–21) is one of the deepest, most profound theological passages in all of Scripture. The nature of humanity's union with Adam and how Adam's sin was transferred to the human race has always been the subject of intense debate. Bible students also disagree on whether 7:7–25 describes Paul's experience as a believer or unbeliever or is a literary device and not intended to be autobiographical at all. The closely related doctrines of election (8:28–30) and the sovereignty of God (9:6–29) have confused many believers. Others question whether chapters 9—11 teach that God has a future plan for the nation of Israel. Some have ignored Paul's teaching on the believer's obedience to human government (13:1–7) in the name of Christian activism, while others have used it to defend slavish obedience to totalitarian regimes.

All of these and more interpretive challenges are addressed in the lessons that follow.

The Good News

Opening Thought

1) What's the *worst* news you've received in the last year? How did you react to this discovery emotionally, physically, etc.?

_____

_____

_____

_____

_____

_____

2) What's the *best* news you've heard in the last year? What was your response?

_____

_____

_____

_____

_____

_____

_____

_____

Background of the Passage

Newspapers, news magazines, and television news shows contain constant reminders that most news is bad and seems to be getting worse. What happens on a national and worldwide scale, however, is simply the magnification of what is occurring on an individual level. As personal problems, animosities, and fears increase, so do their counterparts in society at large.

A terrifying power grips human beings at the very core of their being. Left unchecked, it pushes them to self-destruction in one form or another. That power is sin, and that is always bad news.

The tidbits of good news are often merely brief respites from the bad. And sometimes what appears to be good merely masks an evil. One cynic commented that peace treaties merely provide time for both sides to reload.

The essence of Paul's letter to the Romans, however, is that there is good news that is truly good. The apostle was, in fact, "a minister of Jesus Christ to the Gentiles, ministering the gospel of God" (Romans 15:16). He brought the good news that in Christ sin can be forgiven, selfishness can be overcome, guilt can be removed, anxiety can be alleviated, and people can, indeed, have hope and eternal glory.

The entire thrust of the sixteen chapters of Romans is distilled into the first seven verses. The apostle apparently was so overjoyed by his message of good news that he could not wait to introduce his readers to the gist of what he had to say. He burst into it immediately.

Bible Passage

Read 1:1–17, noting the key words and definitions to the right of the passage.

Romans 1:1–17

¹ *Paul, a bondservant of Jesus Christ, called [to be] an apostle, separated to the gospel of God*

² *which He promised before through His prophets in the Holy Scriptures,*

³ *concerning His Son Jesus Christ our Lord, who was*

bondservant (v. 1)—the Greek word for servant or slave, but given a Hebrew sense here by Paul to imply willing service for a beloved, respected master

born of the seed of David according to the flesh,

4 [and] declared [to be] the Son of God with power according to the Spirit of holiness, by the resurrection from the dead.

5 Through Him we have received grace and apostleship for obedience to the faith among all nations for His name,

6 among whom you also are the called of Jesus Christ;

7 To all who are in Rome, beloved of God, called [to be] saints: Grace to you and peace from God our Father and the Lord Jesus Christ.

8 First, I thank my God through Jesus Christ for you all, that your faith is spoken of throughout the whole world.

9 For God is my witness, whom I serve with my spirit in the gospel of His Son, that without ceasing I make mention of you always in my prayers,

10 making request if, by some means, now at last I may find a way in the will of God to come to you.

11 For I long to see you, that I may impart to you some spiritual gift, so that you may be established—

12 that is, that I may be encouraged together with you by the mutual faith both of you and me.

13 Now I do not want you to be unaware, brethren, that I often planned to come to you (but was hindered until now), that I might have some fruit among you also, just as among the other Gentiles.

14 I am a debtor both to Greeks and to barbarians, both to wise and to unwise.

15 So, as much as is in me, [I am] ready to preach the gospel to you who are in Rome also.

16 For I am not ashamed of the gospel of Christ, for it is the power of God to salvation for everyone who believes, for the Jew first and also for the Greek.

17 For in it the righteousness of God is revealed from faith to faith; as it is written, "The just shall live by faith."

apostle (v. 1)—Literally, "one who is sent;" this title was given to Christ's original twelve disciples, then to Matthaias (Acts 1:15–26); Paul was chosen by Christ to serve in this way (Acts 22:14).

separated to (v. 1)—Paul had been set apart (that is, specially selected) by God for his ministry to the Gentiles.

gospel of God (v. 1)—Gospel means "good news."

declared (v. 4)—Literally, "to distinguish, or mark off," this is the Greek word from which the English word "horizon" comes; as the horizon marks clearly the boundary between earth and sky, the resurrection marks Christ as the Son of God come in the flesh.

obedience to the faith (v. 5)—True saving faith always produces obedience and submission to the Lordship of Christ.

serve with my spirit (v. 9)—The word translated serve can also be translated worship.

spiritual gift (v. 11)—The Greek word for "gift" is charisma and means a *gift of grace*, a divine enablement.

debtor (v. 14)—under obligation to fulfill his ministry because of God's calling and the Gentiles' great need

salvation (v. 16)—deliverance or rescue, in this case from lostness, that is, separation from God

believes (v. 16)—trusts, relies on, or has faith in

Understanding the Text

3) What does this passage reveal about the promise of the Good News (v. 2) and the Person of the Good News (vv. 3, 4)?

_____

_____

_____

_____

4) Verses 8–15 provide interesting insights into Paul's character and motives, as well as the kind of behavior that should mark all true spiritual leaders. What admirable qualities do you see in these verses?

_____

_____

_____

_____

(verses to consider: 1 Thessalonians 2:1—3:13)

5) What reasons does Paul give for not being ashamed of the gospel?

_____

_____

_____

_____

Cross-Reference

Read about Paul's own experience with the Good News and his commissioning by Christ to the Gospel ministry. This testimony is from Acts 26.

¹ *Then Agrippa said to Paul, "You are permitted to speak for yourself." So Paul stretched out his hand and answered for himself:*

2 *"I think myself happy, King Agrippa, because today I shall answer for myself before you concerning all the things of which I am accused by the Jews,*

3 *"especially because you are expert in all customs and questions which have to do with the Jews. Therefore I beg you to hear me patiently.*

4 *"My manner of life from my youth, which was spent from the beginning among my own nation at Jerusalem, all the Jews know.*

5 *"They knew me from the first, if they were willing to testify, that according to the strictest sect of our religion I lived a Pharisee.*

6 *"And now I stand and am judged for the hope of the promise made by God to our fathers.*

7 *"To this [promise] our twelve tribes, earnestly serving [God] night and day, hope to attain. For this hope's sake, King Agrippa, I am accused by the Jews.*

8 *"Why should it be thought incredible by you that God raises the dead?*

9 *"Indeed, I myself thought I must do many things contrary to the name of Jesus of Nazareth.*

10 *"This I also did in Jerusalem, and many of the saints I shut up in prison, having received authority from the chief priests; and when they were put to death, I cast my vote against [them].*

11 *"And I punished them often in every synagogue and compelled [them] to blaspheme; and being exceedingly enraged against them, I persecuted [them] even to foreign cities.*

12 *"While thus occupied, as I journeyed to Damascus with authority and commission from the chief priests,*

13 *"at midday, O king, along the road I saw a light from heaven, brighter than the sun, shining around me and those who journeyed with me.*

14 *"And when we all had fallen to the ground, I heard a voice speaking to me and saying in the Hebrew language, 'Saul, Saul, why are you persecuting Me? [It is] hard for you to kick against the goads.'*

15 *"So I said, 'Who are You, Lord?' And He said, 'I am Jesus, whom you are persecuting.*

16 *'But rise and stand on your feet; for I have appeared to you for this purpose, to make you a minister and a witness both of the things which you have seen and of the things which I will yet reveal to you.*

17 *'I will deliver you from the [Jewish] people, as well as [from] the Gentiles, to whom I now send you,*

18 *'to open their eyes, [in order] to turn [them] from darkness to light, and [from] the power of Satan to God, that they may receive forgiveness of sins and an inheritance among those who are sanctified by faith in Me.'"*

Exploring the Meaning

6) How did Paul's encounter with the risen Christ alter his life and purpose?

_____

_____

_____

_____

7) Read Philippians 3:1–7. What about Paul's life before Christ would have caused him to see the message of Christ as "good news"?

_____

_____

_____

_____

8) What was behind Paul's eagerness to travel widely and minister to others?

_____

_____

_____

_____

Summing Up . . .

"Some people object to terms such as *salvation* and *being saved*, claiming that the ideas they convey are out of date and meaningless to contemporary men and women. But salvation is God's term, and there is no better one to describe what He offers fallen humankind through the sacrifice of His Son. Through Christ, and Christ alone, people can be saved from sin, from Satan, from judgment, from wrath, and from spiritual death."—*John MacArthur*

Reflecting on the Text

9) The dying words of one ancient saint were, "Grace is the only thing that can make us like God. I might be dragged through heaven, earth, and hell and I would still be the same sinful, polluted wretch unless God Himself should cleanse me by His grace."

How would you answer the question of a person who says, "I keep hearing about 'the grace of God.' What does that mean, and why is it such a good thing?"

_____

_____

_____

_____

10) Readers of Paul's letters, especially his conversion story, are struck by his sheer excitement. This man was bowled over, quite literally, by the love of God, and he never seemed to get over God's amazing grace.

How can blah, ho-hum Christians recapture a sense that the Gospel is good news, indeed the very best news ever announced?

_____

_____

_____

_____

11) Who in your life needs to hear and embrace God's good news of salvation by grace through faith in Christ?

_____

_____

_____

_____

Recording Your Thoughts

_____

_____

_____

_____

_____

_____

_____

_____

_____

_____

_____

_____

_____

_____

_____

_____

_____

_____

For further study, see the following passages:

2 Samuel 7:12	Luke 1:35	John 6:44
Acts 1:15–26	Acts 21:11–14, 28	1 Corinthians 9:16–17, 23
1 Corinthians 15:1–4	2 Corinthians 5:21	2 Corinthians 12:9–10
Ephesians 2:8–9	Philippians 4:22	2 Thessalonians 2:13–14
1 Timothy 6:17	Titus 1:11	1 Peter 5:3–4

Opening Thought

1) In an age of tolerance (and twisted logic) such as we live in, to speak of God's wrath and judgment is to invite the wrath and judgment of all those who do not wish to hear the truth of the Scripture.

What would you say to a sincere, concerned friend who argued:

"I just don't think we need to try to scare people into heaven with all this talk of fire and brimstone. Christians should be more positive and emphasize all the blessings of the Christian life, not threaten people with hell, fire, and damnation. It just gives us— and God—a bad name!"

Background of the Passage

After stating the thesis of his epistle—a righteous God is able to make sinners righteous through faith (1:16–17), Paul expounds on the wretchedness of the human heart, and the divine wrath that this rebelliousness elicits.

For Paul, fear of eternal condemnation was the first motivation he offered for coming to Christ, the first pressure he applied to evil men. He was determined that they understand the reality of being under God's wrath before he offered them the way of escape from it. This approach makes both logical and theological sense. A person cannot appreciate the wonder of God's grace until he or she knows about the perfect demands of God's law, and that person cannot appreciate the fullness of God's love until he or she knows something about the fierceness of God's anger against his or her sinful failure to perfectly obey that law. The person cannot appreciate God's forgiveness until he or she knows about the eternal consequences of the sins that require a penalty and need forgiving.

Everyone—Gentiles and Jews, indeed all of humankind—stands guilty before a holy God. Human nature is corrupt. Human thoughts and actions are vile. Human motives are impure. By the time Paul is finished with his divine indictment, every mouth has been shut (3:19–20). We are without excuse. We are incapable of saving ourselves.

This bad news is the necessary first part of the good news called the Gospel.

Bible Passage

Read 1:18—3:20, noting the key words and definitions to the right of the passage.

Romans 1:18—3:20

¹⁸ *For the wrath of God is revealed from heaven against all ungodliness and unrighteousness of men, who suppress the truth in unrighteousness,*

¹⁹ *because what may be known of God is manifest in them, for God has shown [it] to them.*

²⁰ *For since the creation of the world His invisible [attributes] are clearly seen, being understood by the things that are made, [even] His eternal power and Godhead, so that they are without excuse,*

wrath of God (v. 18)—not a capricious, impulsive, arbitrary outburst of anger, but the settled determined response of a holy God against sin

manifest in them (v. 19)— God's sovereignly implanted evidence of His own existence in the heart of every person

21 because, although they knew God, they did not glorify [Him] as God, nor were thankful, but became futile in their thoughts, and their foolish hearts were darkened.

22 Professing to be wise, they became fools,

23 and changed the glory of the incorruptible God into an image made like corruptible man—and birds and four-footed animals and creeping things.

24 Therefore God also gave them up to uncleanness, in the lusts of their hearts, to dishonor their bodies among themselves,

25 who exchanged the truth of God for the lie, and worshipped and served the creature rather than the Creator, who is blessed forever. Amen.

26 For this reason God gave them up to vile passions. For even their women exchanged the natural use for what is against nature.

27 Likewise also the men, leaving the natural use of the woman, burned in their lust for one another, men with men committing what is shameful, and receiving in themselves the penalty of their error which was due.

28 And even as they did not like to retain God in [their] knowledge, God gave them over to a debased mind, to do those things which are not fitting;

29 being filled with all unrighteousness, sexual immorality, wickedness, covetousness, maliciousness; full of envy, murder, strife, deceit, evil-mindedness; [they are] whisperers,

30 backbiters, haters of God, violent, proud, boasters, inventors of evil things, disobedient to parents,

31 undiscerning, untrustworthy, unloving, unforgiving, unmerciful;

32 who, knowing the righteous judgment of God, that those who practice such things are deserving of death, not only do the same but also approve of those who practice them.

1 Therefore you are inexcusable, O man, whoever you are who judge, for in whatever you judge

although they knew God (v. 21)—Every person is conscious of God's existence, power, and divine nature via general revelation.

glorify (v. 21)—honor; We were created for no other reason than to exalt God, the failure or refusal to do so is the ultimate affront to our Creator.

changed the glory . . . into an image (v. 23)—the worship of idols

gave them up (vv. 24, 26) . . . **gave them over** (v. 28)—a Greek judicial term meaning to lord over a prisoner to his sentence; it conveys the sense of abandonment

the lie (v. 25)—the denying of God's existence

vile passions (v. 26)—disgraceful or degrading perversions (for example, in this context, homosexuality)

another you condemn yourself; for you who judge practice the same things.

2 But we know that the judgment of God is according to truth against those who practice such things.

3 And do you think this, O man, you who judge those practicing such things, and doing the same, that you will escape the judgment of God?

4 Or do you despise the riches of His goodness, forbearance, and longsuffering, not knowing that the goodness of God leads you to repentance?

5 But in accordance with your hardness and your impenitent heart you are treasuring up for yourself wrath in the day of wrath and revelation of the righteous judgment of God,

6 who "will render to each one according to his deeds":

7 eternal life to those who by patient continuance in doing good seek for glory, honor, and immortality;

8 but to those who are self-seeking and do not obey the truth, but obey unrighteousness—indignation and wrath,

9 tribulation and anguish, on every soul of man who does evil, of the Jew first and also of the Greek;

10 but glory, honor, and peace to everyone who works what is good, to the Jew first and also to the Greek.

11 For there is no partiality with God.

12 For as many as have sinned without law will also perish without law, and as many as have sinned in the law will be judged by the law

13 (for not the hearers of the law [are] just in the sight of God, but the doers of the law will be justified;

14 for when Gentiles, who do not have the law, by nature do the things in the law, these, although not having the law, are a law to themselves,

15 who show the work of the law written in their hearts, their conscience also bearing witness, and between themselves [their] thoughts accusing or else excusing [them])

16 in the day when God will judge the secrets of men by Jesus Christ, according to my gospel.

despise (2:4)—to think down on to treat with contempt

repentance (v. 4)—the act of turning from sin to Christ for forgiveness

hardness (v. 5)—the Greek word from which we get "sclerosis," that is, a hardening of one's heart

eternal life (v. 7)—not just quantity but an endless quality of existence

partiality (v. 11)—literally, to "receive a face," that is, to give consideration to someone simply because of position, wealth, appearance, and so forth

by nature (v. 14) . . . **conscience** (v. 15)—our God-given instinctive or innate sense of what is right and wrong

17 Indeed you are called a Jew, and rest on the law, and make your boast in God,

18 and know [His] will, and approve the things that are excellent, being instructed out of the law,

19 and are confident that you yourself are a guide to the blind, a light to those who are in darkness,

20 an instructor of the foolish, a teacher of babes, having the form of knowledge and truth in the law.

21 You, therefore, who teach another, do you not teach yourself? You who preach that a man should not steal, do you steal?

22 You who say, "Do not commit adultery," do you commit adultery? You who abhor idols, do you rob temples?

23 You who make your boast in the law, do you dishonor God through breaking the law?

24 For "the name of God is blasphemed among the Gentiles because of you," as it is written.

25 For circumcision is indeed profitable if you keep the law; but if you are a breaker of the law, your circumcision has become uncircumcision.

26 Therefore, if an uncircumcised man keeps the righteous requirements of the law, will not his uncircumcision be counted as circumcision?

27 And will not the physically uncircumcised, if he fulfills the law, judge you who, [even] with [your] written [code] and circumcision, [are] a transgressor of the law?

28 For he is not a Jew who [is one] outwardly, nor [is] circumcision that which [is] outward in the flesh;

29 but [he is] a Jew who [is one] inwardly; and circumcision [is that] of the heart, in the Spirit, not in the letter; whose praise [is] not from men but from God.

1 What advantage then has the Jew, or what [is] the profit of circumcision?

2 Much in every way! Chiefly because to them were committed the oracles of God.

3 For what if some did not believe? Will their unbelief make the faithfulness of God without effect?

---

he is a Jew (v. 29)—The true child of God has a heart separated from sin unto God.

oracles (3:2)—important supernatural sayings or messages

4 *Certainly not! Indeed, let God be true but every man a liar. As it is written: "That You may be justified in Your words, And may overcome when You are judged."*

5 *But if our unrighteousness demonstrates the righteousness of God, what shall we say? [Is] God unjust who inflicts wrath? (I speak as a man.)*

6 *Certainly not! For then how will God judge the world?*

7 *For if the truth of God has increased through my lie to His glory, why am I also still judged as a sinner?*

8 *And [why] not [say], "Let us do evil that good may come"?—as we are slanderously reported and as some affirm that we say. Their condemnation is just.*

9 *What then? Are we better [than they]? Not at all. For we have previously charged both Jews and Greeks that they are all under sin.*

10 *As it is written: "There is none righteous, no, not one;*

11 *There is none who understands; There is none who seeks after God.*

12 *They have all turned aside; They have together become unprofitable; There is none who does good, no, not one."*

13 *"Their throat [is] an open tomb; With their tongues they have practiced deceit"; "The poison of asps [is] under their lips";*

14 *"Whose mouth [is] full of cursing and bitterness."*

15 *"Their feet [are] swift to shed blood;*

16 *Destruction and misery [are] in their ways;*

17 *And the way of peace they have not known."*

18 *"There is no fear of God before their eyes."*

19 *Now we know that whatever the law says, it says to those who are under the law, that every mouth may be stopped, and all the world may become guilty before God.*

20 *Therefore by the deeds of the law no flesh will be justified in His sight, for by the law [is] the knowledge of sin.*

I speak as a man (v. 5)—Paul is paraphrasing the weak, unbiblical logic of his opponents.

we (v. 9)—the Christians in Rome

under sin (v. 9)—enslaved and dominated by sin

unprofitable (v. 12)—useless, worthless; the Hebrew equivalent was used to describe milk that had become rancid

cursing (v. 14)—caustically, derisively wishing the worst for someone

every mouth may be stopped (v. 19)—People are silent and speechless before God's righteous judgment.

Understanding the Text

2) What reasons does Paul give for the wrath of God against men?

_____

_____

_____

> *Circle all the words and descriptive phrases in this*
> *passage for man's rebellion against God.*

3) Other than long-term judgment, what short-term consequences of rebelliousness does Paul cite in this extended passage?

_____

_____

_____

_____

4) According to this passage, why are not even "moral" and religious people exempted from God's widespread judgment?

_____

_____

_____

Cross-Reference

Read Psalm 14 and note how it relates to the above passage in Romans.

¹ *To the Chief Musician. A Psalm of David. The fool has said in his heart,*
"[There is] no God." They are corrupt, They have done abominable works, There
is none who does good.
² *The LORD looks down from heaven upon the children of men, To see if there are*
any who understand, who seek God.

³ *They have all turned aside, They have together become corrupt; [There is] none who does good, No, not one.*

⁴ *Have all the workers of iniquity no knowledge, Who eat up my people [as] they eat bread, And do not call on the LORD?*

⁵ *There they are in great fear, For God [is] with the generation of the righteous.*

⁶ *You shame the counsel of the poor, But the LORD [is] his refuge.*

⁷ *Oh, that the salvation of Israel [would come] out of Zion! When the LORD brings back the captivity of His people, Let Jacob rejoice [and] Israel be glad.*

Exploring the Meaning

5) How do these passages from both Old and New Testaments answer the popular, modern-day belief that "human beings are basically good"?

_____

_____

_____

_____

6) What specific evidence do you see in this passage to suggest that God is not impressed by mere "religious activity"?

_____

_____

_____

_____

7) Read Galatians 3:19–25. Why did God give sinful human beings a perfect law code to follow?

_____

_____

_____

_____

Summing Up . . .

"The final verdict, then, is that unredeemed humankind has no defense what-ever and is guilty of all charges. The defense must rest, as it were, before it has opportunity to say anything, because the omniscient and all-wise God has infallibly demonstrated the impossibility of any grounds for acquittal. "Absolute silence is the only possible response just as there will be utter silence in heaven when the Lord Jesus Christ will one day break the seventh seal and release the seven trumpet judgments upon the condemned earth (see Revelation 8:1–6)."—*John MacArthur*

Reflecting on the Text

8) R. A. Torrey wrote this:
"Shallow views of sin and of God's holiness, and of the glory of Jesus Christ and His claims upon us, lie at the bottom of weak theories of the doom of the impenitent. When we see sin in all its hideousness and enormity, the Holiness of God in all its perfection, and the glory of Jesus Christ in all its infinity, nothing but a doctrine that those who persist in . . . the rejection of the Son of God, shall endure everlasting anguish, will satisfy the demands of our own moral intuitions."

How can a Christian come to a deeper and more accurate understanding of the depravity of the human heart and the holiness of our God?

_____

_____

_____

9) What in this study convicts you most? challenges you most? compels you to action the most? Why?

_____

_____

_____

_____

10) Write a prayer of thanks to God for sparing you from wrath and judgment and for forgiving your sin:

_____

_____

_____

_____

_____

_____

Recording Your Thoughts

_____

_____

_____

_____

_____

_____

_____

For further study, see the following passages:

Exodus 20:3–5	Leviticus 18:22	Deuteronomy 10:16; 30:6
Judges 10:13	Psalm 2:5	Psalm 5:9
Psalm 14:1	Psalm 19:1–8	Psalm 36:1
Isaiah 43:7	Jeremiah 25:15–16	Matthew 23:24–28
John 12:40	John 17:3	Acts 8:26–39
Acts 10:34	1 Corinthians 6:9–11	1 Corinthians 10:31
2 Corinthians 7:9, 11	Galatians 3:10, 13	Galatians 6:7–8
1 Timothy 4:2, 10	Titus 1:1	Hebrews 6:4–6
Hebrews 10:26, 29	Revelation 20:11–15	

By Faith Alone

Opening Thought

1) Think of the people you know (or have observed) from various religious faiths. What are some of the different prescriptions they are following in their attempts to please God or find eternal life?

How much peace of mind do these people seem to have?

What's the problem with trying to *do* things in order to earn favor with God?

_____

_____

_____

_____

_____

_____

_____

_____

_____

_____

_____

_____

_____

Background of the Passage

In the Iliad of Homer, the great Trojan warrior, Hector, was preparing to fight Achilles and the invading Greeks. As he was about to leave home, Hector wanted to hold his young son Astayanax in his arms and bid him farewell for what ended up being the last time. But Hector's armor so frightened the infant that he shrank back to his nurse's caress. The father, laughing out loud then removed his bronze helmet and took up his little child in his arms. The boy discovered the father of his love behind all that armor.

That is similar to what Paul does in his letter to the Romans, beginning with 3:21. Having shown God as judge and executioner, as it were, he next shows the God of love, who reaches out with open arms to sinful people in the hope that they will come to Him and be saved.

After conclusively proving the universal sinfulness of humanity and their desperate need for righteousness (1:18—3:20), Paul shifts gears and demonstrates that God alone can provide that righteousness.

To illustrate this truth, Paul devotes the entire fourth chapter to Abraham. This godly Old Testament saint is a shining example of the central biblical truth that a person can become right with God only by faith in response to His grace, never by works.

Bible Passage

Read 3:21—4:25, noting the key words and definitions to the right of the passage.

Romans 3:21—4:25

²¹ *But now the righteousness of God apart from the law is revealed, being witnessed by the Law and the Prophets,*

²² *even the righteousness of God, through faith in Jesus Christ, to all and on all who believe. For there is no difference;*

²³ *for all have sinned and fall short of the glory of God,*

But (v. 21)—an adversative, contrasting humanity's total depravity and inability to please God, and God's own provision of a way to Himself

²⁴ *being justified freely by His grace through the redemption that is in Christ Jesus,*

²⁵ *whom God set forth [as] a propitiation by His blood, through faith, to demonstrate His righteousness, because in His forbearance God had passed over the sins that were previously committed,*

²⁶ *to demonstrate at the present time His righteousness, that He might be just and the justifier of the one who has faith in Jesus.*

²⁷ *Where [is] boasting then? It is excluded. By what law? Of works? No, but by the law of faith.*

²⁸ *Therefore we conclude that a man is justified by faith apart from the deeds of the law.*

²⁹ *Or [is He] the God of the Jews only? [Is He] not also the God of the Gentiles? Yes, of the Gentiles also,*

³⁰ *since [there is] one God who will justify the circumcised by faith and the uncircumcised through faith.*

³¹ *Do we then make void the law through faith? Certainly not! On the contrary, we establish the law.*

¹ *What then shall we say that Abraham our father has found according to the flesh?*

² *For if Abraham was justified by works, he has [something] to boast about, but not before God.*

³ *For what does the Scripture say? "Abraham believed God, and it was accounted to him for righteousness."*

⁴ *Now to him who works, the wages are not counted as grace but as debt.*

⁵ *But to him who does not work but believes on Him who justifies the ungodly, his faith is accounted for righteousness,*

⁶ *just as David also describes the blessedness of the man to whom God imputes righteousness apart from works:*

⁷ *"Blessed [are those] whose lawless deeds are forgiven, And whose sins are covered;*

justified (v. 24)—a forensic term meaning "to declare righteous"

propitiation (v. 25)—appeasement or satisfaction; Christ's death satisfied the offended holiness of God

passed over (v. 25)—a temporary withholding of judgment

accounted (4:3)—a word used in legal and financial settings; here to take something that belongs to someone and credit it to the account of another

David (v. 5)—King David's sin with Bathsheba is another Old Testament example of imputed righteousness.

justifies the ungodly (v. 5)—Only those who freely admit their unworthiness are candidates for salvation.

8 Blessed [is the] man to whom the LORD shall not impute sin."

9 [Does] this blessedness then [come] upon the circumcised [only], or upon the uncircumcised also? For we say that faith was accounted to Abraham for righteousness.

10 How then was it accounted? While he was circumcised, or uncircumcised? Not while circumcised, but while uncircumcised.

11 And he received the sign of circumcision, a seal of the righteousness of the faith which [he had while still] uncircumcised, that he might be the father of all those who believe, though they are uncircumcised, that righteousness might be imputed to them also,

12 and the father of circumcision to those who not only [are] of the circumcision, but who also walk in the steps of the faith which our father Abraham [had while still] uncircumcised.

13 For the promise that he would be the heir of the world [was] not to Abraham or to his seed through the law, but through the righteousness of faith.

14 For if those who are of the law [are] heirs, faith is made void and the promise made of no effect,

15 because the law brings about wrath; for where there is no law [there is] no transgression.

16 Therefore [it is] of faith that [it might be] according to grace, so that the promise might be sure to all the seed, not only to those who are of the law, but also to those who are of the faith of Abraham, who is the father of us all

17 (as it is written, "I have made you a father of many nations") in the presence of Him whom he believed—God, who gives life to the dead and calls those things which do not exist as though they did;

18 who, contrary to hope, in hope believed, so that he became the father of many nations, according to what was spoken, "So shall your descendants be."

19 And not being weak in faith, he did not consider his own body, already dead (since he was about a hun-

the sign of circumcision
(v. 11)—the physical, racial mark of identity for the Jewish people

walk in the steps (v. 12)—those non-Jews who emulate Abraham's faith

faith is made void and the promise made of no effect (v. 14)—Paul is demonstrating that if adherence to the Law could save, then faith in God's promise would be worthless.

weak in faith (v. 19)—to allow doubt to erode and undermine belief

dred years old), and the deadness of Sarah's womb.

20 He did not waver at the promise of God through unbelief, but was strengthened in faith, giving glory to God,

21 and being fully convinced that what He had promised He was also able to perform.

22 And therefore "it was accounted to him for righteousness."

23 Now it was not written for his sake alone that it was imputed to him,

24 but also for us. It shall be imputed to us who believe in Him who raised up Jesus our Lord from the dead,

25 who was delivered up because of our offenses, and was raised because of our justification.

delivered up (v. 25)—to be crucified as punishment for human beings' sins

Understanding the Text

2) Why does Paul argue that, when it comes to one's standing before God, no one has the right to boast or be filled with religious pride?

_____

_____

_____

_____

> *Circle every word or phrase in this passage that describes what God has done.*

3) Paul goes to some lengths to demonstrate that Abraham was justified in the sight of God long before he was ever circumcised. Why was this an important argument for him to make to his Roman audience?

_____

_____

_____

4) What is the purpose or effect of God's law (4:13–15)?

_____

_____

_____

_____

> *Underline every reference in the passage to God's law.*

Cross-Reference

Read Galatians 3:6–25, noting the parallels with 3:21—4:25:

Galatians 3:6–25

⁶ *just as Abraham "believed God, and it was accounted to him for righteousness."*

⁷ *Therefore know that [only] those who are of faith are sons of Abraham.*

⁸ *And the Scripture, foreseeing that God would justify the Gentiles by faith, preached the gospel to Abraham beforehand, [saying], "In you all the nations shall be blessed."*

⁹ *So then those who [are] of faith are blessed with believing Abraham.*

¹⁰ *For as many as are of the works of the law are under the curse; for it is written, "Cursed [is] everyone who does not continue in all things which are written in the book of the law, to do them."*

¹¹ *But that no one is justified by the law in the sight of God [is] evident, for "the just shall live by faith."*

¹² *Yet the law is not of faith, but "the man who does them shall live by them."*

¹³ *Christ has redeemed us from the curse of the law, having become a curse for us (for it is written, "Cursed [is] everyone who hangs on a tree"),*

¹⁴ *that the blessing of Abraham might come upon the Gentiles in Christ Jesus, that we might receive the promise of the Spirit through faith.*

¹⁵ *Brethren, I speak in the manner of men: Though [it is] only a man's covenant, yet [if it is] confirmed, no one annuls or adds to it.*

¹⁶ *Now to Abraham and his Seed were the promises made. He does not say, "And to seeds," as of many, but as of one, "And to your Seed," who is Christ.*

¹⁷ *And this I say, [that] the law, which was four hundred and thirty years later, cannot annul the covenant that was confirmed before by God in Christ, that it should make the promise of no effect.*

18 *For if the inheritance [is] of the law, [it is] no longer of promise; but God gave [it] to Abraham by promise.*

19 *What purpose then [does] the law [serve]? It was added because of transgressions, till the Seed should come to whom the promise was made; [and it was] appointed through angels by the hand of a mediator.*

20 *Now a mediator does not [mediate] for one [only], but God is one.*

21 *[Is] the law then against the promises of God? Certainly not! For if there had been a law given which could have given life, truly righteousness would have been by the law.*

22 *But the Scripture has confined all under sin, that the promise by faith in Jesus Christ might be given to those who believe.*

23 *But before faith came, we were kept under guard by the law, kept for the faith which would afterward be revealed.*

24 *Therefore the law was our tutor [to bring us] to Christ, that we might be justified by faith.*

25 *But after faith has come, we are no longer under a tutor.*

Exploring the Meaning

5) How does Galatians 3 underscore Paul's argument in chapters 3 and 4?

_____

_____

_____

_____

_____

6) What incidents from the life of Abraham and Sarah does Paul use to make the case that salvation is by divine power, not human effort?

_____

_____

_____

_____

_____

7) Read 2 Corinthians 5:21. If God's wrath is directed toward unrighteousness, and His favor is directed toward righteousness, what are the wonderful implications of this verse for believers?

_____

_____

_____

_____

_____

Summing Up . . .

"Scripture makes clear that there is indeed a way to God, but that it is not based on anything men themselves can do to achieve or merit it. Man can be made right with God, but not on his own terms or in his own power. In that basic regard Christianity is distinct from every other religion. As far as the way of salvation is concerned, there are therefore only two religions the world has ever known or will ever know—the religion of divine accomplishment, which is biblical Christianity, and the religion of human achievement, which includes all other kinds of religion, by whatever names they may go under."—*John MacArthur*

Reflecting on the Text

8) Some Christians view God's law and His grace as contradictory. Based on what you have seen in this lesson, how would you harmonize these two truths?

_____

_____

_____

_____

_____

9) If salvation were by human effort, we could boast. Since salvation is all of grace, what is the proper response of the redeemed?

_____

_____

_____

_____

_____

10) What friends, neighbors, and family members do not yet understand the concept of righteousness by faith? Pray that God will open their eyes to this truth.

_____

_____

_____

_____

_____

Recording Your Thoughts

_____

_____

_____

_____

_____

_____

_____

_____

For further study, see the following passages:

Genesis 15:6   Isaiah 53:4–5, 12   Luke 5:32
Acts 17:30–31   1 Corinthians 1:26–30   1 Corinthians 3:21–23
2 Corinthians 5:21   Galatians 2:16   Galatians 3:6–7, 24, 29
Colossians 2:11–14   1 Timothy 2:6   Titus 3:5

Additional Notes

_____

_____

_____

_____

_____

_____

_____

_____

_____

_____

_____

_____

_____

_____

_____

_____

_____

_____

_____

_____

_____

Blessings & Imputation

Opening Thought

1) What do people do to feel secure?

_____

_____

_____

_____

_____

_____

_____

2) Why is it important to feel secure in one's relationship with God?

_____

_____

_____

_____

_____

_____

_____

_____

_____

Background of the Passage

After describing the appalling sin and lostness of all humankind (1:18—3:20), Paul revealed how Christ, by His justifying death on the cross, has provided the way of salvation for everyone who comes to God in faith (3:21—4:25).

Next, Paul moves to answer two important questions that were, no doubt, on the minds of his readers. First, how complete, or how secure is this salvation provided by Christ? Can we really be certain? What happens if we sin after turning to Christ in faith? Answering this query is the subject of 5:1–11.

The second issue addressed by Paul in 5:12–21 is "How could what one man did at one time in history have such an absolute effect on humankind?" Paul concisely answers this question by comparing the reign of death that Adam's sin engendered with the reign of life made possible by Christ's perfect sacrifice.

Though many people consider the latter half of Romans 5 to be one of the most enigmatic passages in the New Testament, when looked at carefully, this chapter is a source of great comfort and genuine awe in a God who is able and willing to provide such a great salvation.

Bible Passage

Read 5:1–21, noting the key words and definitions to the right of the passage.

Romans 5:1–21

1 *Therefore, having been justified by faith, we have peace with God through our Lord Jesus Christ,*

2 *through whom also we have access by faith into this grace in which we stand, and rejoice in hope of the glory of God.*

3 *And not only [that], but we also glory in tribulations, knowing that tribulation produces perseverance;*

4 *and perseverance, character; and character, hope.*

5 *Now hope does not disappoint, because the love of God has been poured out in our hearts by the Holy Spirit who was given to us.*

having been justified (v. 1)—The Greek construction of this verb indicates a one-time legal declaration with ongoing results.

we have (v. 1)—we presently possess

peace with God (v. 1)—an external, objective reality, not a subjective, internal sense of serenity and calm

access (v. 2)—introduction

6 *For when we were still without strength, in due time Christ died for the ungodly.*

7 *For scarcely for a righteous man will one die; yet perhaps for a good man someone would even dare to die.*

8 *But God demonstrates His own love toward us, in that while we were still sinners, Christ died for us.*

9 *Much more then, having now been justified by His blood, we shall be saved from wrath through Him.*

10 *For if when we were enemies we were reconciled to God through the death of His Son, much more, having been reconciled, we shall be saved by His life.*

11 *And not only [that], but we also rejoice in God through our Lord Jesus Christ, through whom we have now received the reconciliation.*

12 *Therefore, just as through one man sin entered the world, and death through sin, and thus death spread to all men, because all sinned—*

13 *(For until the law sin was in the world, but sin is not imputed when there is no law.*

14 *Nevertheless death reigned from Adam to Moses, even over those who had not sinned according to the likeness of the transgression of Adam, who is a type of Him who was to come.*

15 *But the free gift [is] not like the offense. For if by the one man's offense many died, much more the grace of God and the gift by the grace of the one Man, Jesus Christ, abounded to many.*

16 *And the gift [is] not like [that which came] through the one who sinned. For the judgment [which came] from one [offense resulted] in condemnation, but the free gift [which came] from many offenses [resulted] in justification.*

17 *For if by the one man's offense death reigned through the one, much more those who receive abundance of grace and of the gift of righteousness will reign in life through the One, Jesus Christ.)*

18 *Therefore, as through one man's offense [judgment] came to all men, resulting in condemnation, even*

stand (v. 2)—the idea of permanence, of being fixed and immovable

hope (v. 2)—a certainty not yet realized; not a wishful, uncertain dream

tribulations (v. 3)—extreme pressure, as in the pressure exerted to extract oil from an olive

perseverance (v. 4)—remaining under tremendous weight without succumbing; endurance

character (v. 4)—literally "proof," a term used in the testing of precious metals to determine their purity

poured out (v. 5)—God's love is lavished on His children.

without strength (v. 6)—literally "helpless," because of their spiritual deadness

ungodly (v. 6)—a proof that Christ's love was never based on human merit

because all sinned (v. 12)—All humanity existed in the loins of Adam and have through procreation inherited his fallenness and depravity. Thus it can be said that all sinned in him.

a type of Him . . . to come (v. 14)—Adam and Christ were similar in that their acts affected many others.

death reigned (v. 17)—Adam's sinful act brought universal death.

so through one Man's righteous act [the free gift came] to all men, resulting in justification of life.

¹⁹ For as by one man's disobedience many were made sinners, so also by one Man's obedience many will be made righteous.

²⁰ Moreover the law entered that the offense might abound. But where sin abounded, grace abounded much more,

²¹ so that as sin reigned in death, even so grace might reign through righteousness to eternal life through Jesus Christ our Lord.

Understanding the Text

3) How does Paul refute the erroneous notion that we receive salvation by faith but must preserve it by good works? What evidences does he give that salvation is unconditional?

_____

_____

_____

_____

_____

Circle all the verbs in vv. 1–11, noting especially their tenses.

4) What word picture does Paul use to drive home the truth that unbelievers are actually at war with God?

_____

_____

_____

_____

5) How did Adam's actions affect the human race? What were the affects of Christ's actions?

_____

_____

_____

_____

Cross-Reference

Read the following passage and consider what the author has to say about the law's inability to save us, Christ's perfect sacrifice, and the possibilities this creates for relating to God.

Hebrews 10:1–23

1 *For the law, having a shadow of the good things to come, [and] not the very image of the things, can never with these same sacrifices, which they offer continually year by year, make those who approach perfect.*

2 *For then would they not have ceased to be offered? For the worshipers, once purified, would have had no more consciousness of sins.*

3 *But in those [sacrifices there is] a reminder of sins every year.*

4 *For [it is] not possible that the blood of bulls and goats could take away sins.*

5 *Therefore, when He came into the world, He said: "Sacrifice and offering You did not desire, But a body You have prepared for Me.*

6 *In burnt offerings and [sacrifices] for sin You had no pleasure.*

7 *Then I said, 'Behold, I have come—In the volume of the book it is written of Me—To do Your will, O God.'"*

8 *Previously saying, "Sacrifice and offering, burnt offerings, and [offerings] for sin You did not desire, nor had pleasure [in them]" (which are offered according to the law),*

9 *then He said, "Behold, I have come to do Your will, O God." He takes away the first that He may establish the second.*

10 *By that will we have been sanctified through the offering of the body of Jesus Christ once [for all].*

11 *And every priest stands ministering daily and offering repeatedly the same sacrifices, which can never take away sins.*

¹² But this Man, after He had offered one sacrifice for sins forever, sat down at the right hand of God,

¹³ from that time waiting till His enemies are made His footstool.

¹⁴ For by one offering He has perfected forever those who are being sanctified.

¹⁵ But the Holy Spirit also witnesses to us; for after He had said before,

¹⁶ "This [is] the covenant that I will make with them after those days, says the LORD: I will put My laws into their hearts, and in their minds I will write them,"

¹⁷ [then He adds], "Their sins and their lawless deeds I will remember no more."

¹⁸ Now where there is remission of these, [there is] no longer an offering for sin.

¹⁹ Therefore, brethren, having boldness to enter the Holiest by the blood of Jesus,

²⁰ by a new and living way which He consecrated for us, through the veil, that is, His flesh,

²¹ and [having] a High Priest over the house of God,

²² let us draw near with a true heart in full assurance of faith, having our hearts sprinkled from an evil conscience and our bodies washed with pure water.

²³ Let us hold fast the confession of [our] hope without wavering, for He who promised [is] faithful.

Exploring the Meaning

6) Why do both of these passages (Romans 4; Hebrews 10) make so much about access to God?

_____

_____

_____

_____

7) In what ways does this Hebrews passage echo the idea that salvation is permanent?

_____

_____

_____

_____

8) A doctor once told a hurting patient, "Don't worry. I've got way more medicine than you've got pain." How does this illustrate the truth expressed in 5:20? What is significant about this concept?

_____

_____

_____

_____

Summing Up . . .

"Jesus Christ broke the power of sin and death, but the converse is not true. Sin and death cannot break the power of Jesus Christ. The condemnation of Adam's sin is reversible, the redemption of Jesus Christ is not. The effect of Adam's act is permanent only if not nullified by Christ. The effect of Christ's act, however, is permanent for believing individuals and not subject to reversal or nullification. We have the great assurance that once we are in Jesus Christ, we are in Him forever."—*John MacArthur*

Reflecting on the Text

9) A. W. Pink said the following about eternal security:

"It is utterly and absolutely impossible that the sentence of the divine Judge should ever be revoked or reversed. Sooner shall the lightnings of omnipotence shiver the Rock of Ages than those sheltering in Him again be brought under condemnation."

How does knowing that your salvation is eternally secure affect your life on a daily basis? How does it make you feel?

_____

_____

_____

_____

10) Write a prayer of gratitude to God in response to this lesson.

_____

_____

_____

_____

Recording Your Thoughts

_____

_____

_____

_____

_____

_____

_____

_____

_____

_____

_____

For further study, see the following passages:

Deuteronomy 32:21–22	Psalm 36:5	Psalm 51:5
Matthew 5:10–12	John 3:36	John 7:38–39
Acts 5:28	Galatians 3:19	Ephesians 1:18–20
Ephesians 2:1, 18	Ephesians 3:12, 14–19	Ephesians 5:6
Philippians 1:6	Philippians 3:8–9	2 Thessalonians 1:4
2 Timothy 2:13	Hebrews 7:7–10	Hebrews 9:12
James 1:12		

Dead and Alive!

Opening Thought

1) Some believers are "vampire Christians"; that is, they eagerly want the blood of Christ (to pay for their sins and provide eternal life for them), but they want nothing to do with the life of Christ.

Is this statement true? What's wrong with that kind of thinking?

_____

_____

_____

_____

_____

_____

_____

_____

_____

_____

_____

_____

_____

_____

_____

_____

Background of the Passage

Like a skillful lawyer building an airtight case, the Apostle Paul has been laying out the remarkable facts of the gospel. After an extensive discussion of human beings' sin (and utter inability to please God), Paul announces the doctrine of justification which is God's declaring believing sinners righteous (3:20—5:21).

Next he moves to the subject of the believer's holiness—the life of righteousness that God demands of and provides for His children, the life of obedience to His Word lived in the power of His Spirit. In short, Paul sets out to demonstrate the practical ramifications of salvation for those who have been justified. He specifically begins a lengthy discussion on the doctrine of sanctification, which is God's producing actual righteousness in the believer (6:1—8:39).

Paul addresses the logical conclusion of his readers: If the old self is dead, why is there continually a struggle with sin and how can the new self become dominant? His exhortation is contained in two key words: "reckon" (vv. 11b-12) and "present" (vv. 13–14).

The final section of chapter 6 continues Paul's discussion of sanctification by reminding his readers of their past slavery to sin and their new slavery to righteousness. He wants them to live in submission to their new master, Jesus Christ, and not to be entangled again with the sins that characterized their old life, sins which no longer have any claim over them.

All whom God has justified *will* experience personal holiness.

Bible Passage

Read 6:1–23, noting the key words and definitions to the right of the passage.

Romans 6:1–23

1 *What shall we say then? Shall we continue in sin that grace may abound?*
2 *Certainly not! How shall we who died to sin live any longer in it?*
3 *Or do you not know that as many of us as were baptized into Christ Jesus were baptized into His death?*

Shall we continue in sin . . .
(v. 1)—Paul anticipated that skeptics might reason, "If salvation is based entirely upon grace, won't this encourage license?"

Certainly not! (v. 2)—literally, "may it never be, by no means"; a strong Greek idiom of repudiation

⁴ Therefore we were buried with Him through baptism into death, that just as Christ was raised from the dead by the glory of the Father, even so we also should walk in newness of life.

⁵ For if we have been united together in the likeness of His death, certainly we also shall be [in the likeness] of [His] resurrection,

⁶ knowing this, that our old man was crucified with [Him], that the body of sin might be done away with, that we should no longer be slaves of sin.

⁷ For he who has died has been freed from sin.

⁸ Now if we died with Christ, we believe that we shall also live with Him,

⁹ knowing that Christ, having been raised from the dead, dies no more. Death no longer has dominion over Him.

¹⁰ For [the death] that He died, He died to sin once for all; but [the life] that He lives, He lives to God.

¹¹ Likewise you also, reckon yourselves to be dead indeed to sin, but alive to God in Christ Jesus our Lord.

¹² Therefore do not let sin reign in your mortal body, that you should obey it in its lusts.

¹³ And do not present your members [as] instruments of unrighteousness to sin, but present yourselves to God as being alive from the dead, and your members [as] instruments of righteousness to God.

¹⁴ For sin shall not have dominion over you, for you are not under law but under grace.

¹⁵ What then? Shall we sin because we are not under law but under grace? Certainly not!

¹⁶ Do you not know that to whom you present yourselves slaves to obey, you are that one's slaves whom you obey, whether of sin [leading] to death, or of obedience [leading] to righteousness?

¹⁷ But God be thanked that [though] you were slaves of sin, yet you obeyed from the heart that form of doctrine to which you were delivered.

baptized into Christ Jesus (v. 3)—Not a literal water baptism, but a metaphorical immersion of a person into the work of Christ; that is, completely united and identified with Him, "so as to alter [a person's] condition or relationship to [his or her] previous environment or condition" (Wuest).

newness of life (v. 4)—In the same way that we were united with Christ in his death and burial, so too in His resurrection; this speaks of regeneration.

our old man (v. 6)—a believer's unregenerate self, worn-out and useless

crucified (v. 6)—not merely made to suffer but put to death

body of sin (v. 6)—essentially a synonym for the "old man"

freed from sin (v. 7)—no longer under sin's domination

dominion (v. 9)—mastery, control, or domination

reckon (v. 11)—to count or number; in this sense to have an absolute, unreserved confidence in what one's mind knows to be true, so much so that it affects one's actions and decisions

mortal body (v. 12)—the only remaining repository where sin finds the believer vulnerable

present (v. 13)—refers to a decision of the will

your members (v. 13)—the parts of the physical body from which sin operates in the life of a believer

18 *And having been set free from sin, you became slaves of righteousness.*

19 *I speak in human [terms] because of the weakness of your flesh. For just as you presented your members [as] slaves of uncleanness, and of lawlessness [leading] to [more] lawlessness, so now present your members [as] slaves [of] righteousness for holiness.*

20 *For when you were slaves of sin, you were free in regard to righteousness.*

21 *What fruit did you have then in the things of which you are now ashamed? For the end of those things [is] death.*

22 *But now having been set free from sin, and having become slaves of God, you have your fruit to holiness, and the end, everlasting life.*

23 *For the wages of sin [is] death, but the gift of God [is] eternal life in Christ Jesus our Lord.*

weakness of your flesh
(v. 19)—the human difficulty in grasping divine truth

Understanding the Text

2) How would you summarize Paul's emphatic rejection of the idea that believers in Christ will continue to live as they did when they were unbelievers?

_____

_____

_____

_____

> *Underline the phrases and words that describe the believer's union or identification with Christ.*

3) What does Paul say happened to our old selves?

_____

_____

_____

_____

_____

4) What things do believers need to "know"? How does this "knowing" differ from the "reckoning" (v. 11) that believers are commanded to do?

_____

_____

_____

_____

_____

Cross-Reference

Note the parallels in Colossians 3 with what you've been studying in chapter 6.

Colossians 3:1–11

1 *If then you were raised with Christ, seek those things which are above, where Christ is, sitting at the right hand of God.*

2 *Set your mind on things above, not on things on the earth.*

3 *For you died, and your life is hidden with Christ in God.*

4 *When Christ [who is] our life appears, then you also will appear with Him in glory.*

5 *Therefore put to death your members which are on the earth: fornication, uncleanness, passion, evil desire, and covetousness, which is idolatry.*

6 *Because of these things the wrath of God is coming upon the sons of disobedience,*

7 *in which you yourselves once walked when you lived in them.*

8 *But now you yourselves are to put off all these: anger, wrath, malice, blasphemy, filthy language out of your mouth.*

9 *Do not lie to one another, since you have put off the old man with his deeds,*

10 *and have put on the new [man] who is renewed in knowledge according to the image of Him who created him,*

11 *where there is neither Greek nor Jew, circumcised nor uncircumcised, barbarian, Scythian, slave [nor] free, but Christ [is] all and in all.*

Exploring the Meaning

5) Why does Colossians 3 say that unholy living is improper (and even unthinkable!) for Christians?

_____

_____

_____

_____

6) If Christians really are dead to sin and alive to God, why do we still struggle so with temptation?

_____

_____

_____

_____

7) These passages teach two truths: (1) *God* is the one who changes us—sanctification is by His grace; and yet, (2) in the sanctification process *we* are commanded to do certain things and not do certain things. How do you reconcile these facts?

_____

_____

_____

_____

Summing Up . . .

"Jesus Christ is not looking for people who want to add Him to their sin as an insurance against hell. He is not looking for people who want to apply His high moral principles to their unregenerate lives. He is not looking for those who want only to be outwardly reformed by having their old nature improved.

"Jesus Christ calls to Himself those who are willing to be inwardly transformed by Him, who desire an entirely new nature that is created in His own holy likeness. He calls to Himself those who are willing to die with Him in order to be raised with Him, who are willing to relinquish slavery to their sin for slavery to His righteousness. And when people come to Him on His terms, He changes their destiny from eternal death to eternal life."—*John MacArthur*

Reflecting on the Text

8) The noble theologian Charles Hodge summarized:

"There can be no participation in Christ's life without a participation in his death, and we cannot enjoy the benefits of his death unless we are partakers of the power of his life. We must be reconciled to God in order to be holy, and we cannot be reconciled without thereby becoming holy."

How does this statement address the issue of "vampire Christians" discussed in question 1 of this lesson?

_____

_____

_____

_____

_____

9) In the three-part process of sanctification described in this passage (that is, "know," "reckon," and "present"), where do you sense the greatest struggle? Is it in understanding God's salvation truths, really being convinced by them, or choosing to live them out?

_____

_____

_____

_____

_____

10) What one or two practical applications do you sense the Spirit of God prompting you to employ as a result of this study?

_____

_____

_____

_____

Recording Your Thoughts

_____

_____

_____

_____

_____

_____

_____

_____

_____

_____

_____

For further study, see the following passages:

Ezekiel 36:26	1 Corinthians 6:9–11a, 17	1 Corinthians 9:27
1 Corinthians 15:53	Galatians 2:20	Galatians 3:27
Galatians 6:15	Ephesians 2:8–9	Ephesians 4:2
Philippians 2:12–13	Colossians 3:9–10	1 Timothy 1:8, 12–13
Titus 2:1	Hebrews 7:26–27	1 Peter 2:2
1 Peter 3:18, 21		

Law Abuse

Opening Thought

1) Some churches are libertine or lax in their practice. They abuse the notion of grace and the result is rampant sin. Other churches are legalistic. They misrepresent the notion of grace by piling a heavy load of human-made rules on their parishioners.

While neither extreme is God-honoring or healthy, most individuals and churches tend to lean one way or the other. Which tendency do you typically have to watch out for—liberty or legalism?

What is the appeal of churches/leaders who give their members/followers long lists of "dos and don'ts"?

_____

_____

_____

_____

_____

_____

_____

_____

_____

_____

_____

Background of the Passage

In this doctrinal masterpiece, Paul, the consummate theologian, has first established the sad, sinful state of human beings. All are under *condemnation*. However, the good news includes the miracle of *justification*—a righteousness from God available by grace through faith.

But the gospel received from God and preached by Paul doesn't stop there. It also includes *sanctification*—that truth of absolute identification with Christ (in His death, burial, and resurrection), by which God transforms redeemed sinners into the very likeness of Christ.

Knowing that his readers—especially Jewish ones—would have many questions about how the law relates to their faith in Christ, Paul next sets out to explain that relationship. He also addresses the issue of why believers who are dead to sin still struggle with sinful desires.

To summarize, chapter 7 teaches that the law: (1) can no longer condemn a believer (vv. 1–6); (2) convicts unbelievers (and believers) of sin (vv. 7–13); and (3) cannot deliver a believer from sin (vv. 14–25).

Let's look at this passage in greater detail . . .

Bible Passage

Read 7:1–25, noting the key words and definitions to the right of the passage.

Romans 7:1–25

1 *Or do you not know, brethren (for I speak to those who know the law), that the law has dominion over a man as long as he lives?*

2 *For the woman who has a husband is bound by the law to [her] husband as long as he lives. But if the husband dies, she is released from the law of [her] husband.*

3 *So then if, while [her] husband lives, she marries another man, she will be called an adulteress; but if her husband dies, she is free from that law, so*

dominion (v. 1)—jurisdiction

become dead (v. 4)—literally "you were made to die"; in response to a sinner's faith, God makes the sinner forever dead to the condemnation and penalty of law

married to another (v.4)—united with Christ in a permanent relationship

that she is no adulteress, though she has married another man.

4 Therefore, my brethren, you also have become dead to the law through the body of Christ, that you may be married to another—to Him who was raised from the dead, that we should bear fruit to God.

5 For when we were in the flesh, the sinful passions which were aroused by the law were at work in our members to bear fruit to death.

6 But now we have been delivered from the law, having died to what we were held by, so that we should serve in the newness of the Spirit and not [in] the oldness of the letter.

7 What shall we say then? [Is] the law sin? Certainly not! On the contrary, I would not have known sin except through the law. For I would not have known covetousness unless the law had said, "You shall not covet."

8 But sin, taking opportunity by the commandment, produced in me all [manner of evil] desire. For apart from the law sin [was] dead.

9 I was alive once without the law, but when the commandment came, sin revived and I died.

10 And the commandment, which [was] to [bring] life, I found to [bring] death.

11 For sin, taking occasion by the commandment, deceived me, and by it killed [me].

12 Therefore the law [is] holy, and the commandment holy and just and good.

13 Has then what is good become death to me? Certainly not! But sin, that it might appear sin, was producing death in me through what is good, so that sin through the commandment might become exceedingly sinful.

14 For we know that the law is spiritual, but I am carnal, sold under sin.

15 For what I am doing, I do not understand. For what I will to do, that I do not practice; but what I hate, that I do.

fruit (v. 4)—a transformed life that manifests new attitudes and actions

flesh (v. 5)—people's unredeemed humanness, that is, that remnant of the old man that will remain with each believer until each receives his or her glorified body

sinful passions (v. 5)—the overwhelming impulses to think and do evil

aroused by the law (v. 5)—The unbeliever's rebellious nature is awakened when restrictions are placed on him or her.

fruit to death (v. 5)—Sin brings a harvest of eternal judgment in the life of an unbeliever.

delivered from the law (v. 6)—Because we died in Christ, we are no longer subject to the condemnation and penalties of the law.

oldness of the letter (v. 6)—the external, written law code that produced only condemnation

Is the law sin? (v. 7)—Paul wanted to make sure his readers understood that the law was not imperfect or evil but rather only a beacon to point out evil.

opportunity (v. 8)—a starting point or base of operations

dead (v. 8)—that is, dormant

sin . . . deceived me (v. 11)—by causing people to think they could find life in keeping the law

carnal (v. 14)—Literally, "of flesh"; that is, incarcerated in

16 *If, then, I do what I will not to do, I agree with the law that [it is] good.*

17 *But now, [it is] no longer I who do it, but sin that dwells in me.*

18 *For I know that in me (that is, in my flesh) nothing good dwells; for to will is present with me, but [how] to perform what is good I do not find.*

19 *For the good that I will [to do], I do not do; but the evil I will not [to do], that I practice.*

20 *Now if I do what I will not [to do], it is no longer I who do it, but sin that dwells in me.*

21 *I find then a law, that evil is present with me, the one who wills to do good.*

22 *For I delight in the law of God according to the inward man.*

23 *But I see another law in my members, warring against the law of my mind, and bringing me into captivity to the law of sin which is in my members.*

24 *O wretched man that I am! Who will deliver me from this body of death?*

25 *I thank God—through Jesus Christ our Lord! So then, with the mind I myself serve the law of God, but with the flesh the law of sin.*

unredeemed humanness; Paul is not in the flesh, but the flesh is in him.

sin that dwells in me (v. 17)— Paul's sin flowed not from his new, redeemed nature but from his unredeemed humanness or flesh.

law of my mind (v. 23)—equivalent to the new inner self

deliver (v. 24)—to rescue from danger, as in a soldier pulling his wounded comrade from the battlefield

Understanding the Text

2) What illustration or example does Paul use to explain the manner in which believers are dead to the law?

_____

_____

_____

_____

_____

_____

3) As Paul explains it in chapter 7, what is the connection or relationship between the law and sin? (that is, how does the law *reveal* sin? *arouse* sin?)

_____

_____

_____

_____

_____

> **Underline every reference to the law in this passage.
> Circle words and phrases that speak about sin.**

4) How do we reconcile Paul's discussion of the believer as an entirely new creation, dead to sin, in chapter 6 with his admission of a huge struggle with sin in chapter 7?

_____

_____

_____

_____

Cross-Reference

Note the psalmist's high view of God's law in Psalm 19:7–11:

7 *The law of the* Lord *[is] perfect, converting the soul; The testimony of the* Lord *[is] sure, making wise the simple;*

8 *The statutes of the* Lord *[are] right, rejoicing the heart; The commandment of the* Lord *[is] pure, enlightening the eyes;*

9 *The fear of the* Lord *[is] clean, enduring forever; The judgments of the* Lord *[are] true [and] righteous altogether.*

10 *More to be desired [are they] than gold, Yea, than much fine gold; Sweeter also than honey and the honeycomb.*

11 *Moreover by them Your servant is warned, [And] in keeping them [there is] great reward.*

Exploring the Meaning

5) Is there a contradiction between Paul's observation that the law is a demanding, unyielding code of condemnation and David's obvious affection for the law in Psalm 19? Why or why not?

_____

_____

_____

_____

6) Read 1 Peter 2:11. How does this command echo the internal struggle described by Paul in this passage?

_____

_____

_____

_____

7) Where did Paul ultimately find hope in his struggle against sin and in his inability to live as God commands?

_____

_____

_____

_____

Summing Up . . .

"Sin is so wretched and powerful that, even in a redeemed person, it hangs on and contaminates his living and frustrates his inner desire to obey the wil of God."—*John MacArthur*

Reflecting on the Text

8) Obviously giving in to sinful desires cannot please God or bring about the righteous life that he requires. Based on chapter 7, how effective is legalism in fighting the flesh?

_____

_____

_____

_____

_____

9) What about this passage convicts you? Comforts you? Why?

_____

_____

_____

_____

_____

10) What two things should you be doing that you're not doing? Two things you should not be doing that you are doing? Write those items in the space below and make them a source of prayer in the week to come.

_____

_____

_____

_____

Recording Your Thoughts

_____

_____

_____

_____

_____

_____

_____

_____

_____

_____

_____

_____

_____

_____

_____

_____

_____

_____

_____

_____

_____

_____

For further study, see the following passages:

Psalm 1:2	Psalm 38:14	John 15:1–2
1 Corinthians 7:39	1 Corinthians 15:52–57	2 Corinthians 5:4
2 Corinthians 11:5	Galatians 3:19–22	Galatians 5:6–7, 17, 22–2
Ephesians 2:3	Ephesians 3:16	Ephesians 5:24–27
Philippians 3:7–8	1 Timothy 1:15	

In the Spirit

Romans 8:1–39

Opening Thought

1) Anyone who watches much Christian television programming (especially on those higher-numbered channels) will be introduced to a heavy dose of teaching on the Holy Spirit (or Holy Ghost, as He is often called). The problem with much of this instruction is that it is confusing and at odds with what the Scripture says.

Briefly summarize what the average person thinks of when he or she hears the phrase "Holy Spirit."

_____

_____

_____

_____

_____

_____

_____

_____

_____

_____

_____

_____

Background of the Passage

Having spoken of condemnation (due to human sin) and justification (due to Christ's sacrifice on behalf of sinners), Paul turns next to the vital issues of sanctification (the believer's ongoing struggle with sin) and glorification (transformation into the image of Christ).

In the first seven chapters, God's Holy Spirit is mentioned only once. Now, in chapter 8, Paul mentions the Spirit almost twenty times. It is the Spirit who frees us from sin and death, enables us to fulfill God's law, changes our nature, gives us the ability to overcome the desires of our unredeemed flesh, confirms our adoption as God's children, and guarantees our eternal glory.

In short, there can be no success or progress in the Christian life apart from an utter dependence on the third Person of the Trinity.

Paul closes the chapter with profound teaching about the believer's absolute security. Not only are we saved by the blood of Christ and indwelt by the Spirit, but we also are safe in the Father's love. The God who is in control of all things, who has graciously saved us from sin and death, and who has begun the process of transformation in us, will never let us go.

Bible Passage

Read 8:1–39, noting the key words and definitions to the right of the passage

Romans 8:1–39

¹ [There is] therefore now no condemnation to those who are in Christ Jesus, who do not walk according to the flesh, but according to the Spirit.
² For the law of the Spirit of life in Christ Jesus has made me free from the law of sin and death.
³ For what the law could not do in that it was weak through the flesh, God [did] by sending His own Son in the likeness of sinful flesh, on account of sin: He condemned sin in the flesh,
⁴ that the righteous requirement of the law might be fulfilled in us who do not walk according to the flesh but according to the Spirit.

therefore (v. 1)—Here Paul summarizes the ramifications of the truths presented in chapters 1—7

condemnation (v. 1)—a judicial term meaning a guilty verdict; the opposite of justification

the law of the Spirit of life (v. 2)—the Gospel, the law of faith

the law of sin and death (v. 2)—God's perfect law that, because of the weakness of the flesh, produces only condemnation.

5 *For those who live according to the flesh set their minds on the things of the flesh, but those [who live] according to the Spirit, the things of the Spirit.*

6 *For to be carnally minded [is] death, but to be spiritually minded [is] life and peace.*

7 *Because the carnal mind [is] enmity against God; for it is not subject to the law of God, nor indeed can be.*

8 *So then, those who are in the flesh cannot please God.*

9 *But you are not in the flesh but in the Spirit, if indeed the Spirit of God dwells in you. Now if anyone does not have the Spirit of Christ, he is not His.*

10 *And if Christ [is] in you, the body [is] dead because of sin, but the Spirit [is] life because of righteousness.*

11 *But if the Spirit of Him who raised Jesus from the dead dwells in you, He who raised Christ from the dead will also give life to your mortal bodies through His Spirit who dwells in you.*

12 *Therefore, brethren, we are debtors—not to the flesh, to live according to the flesh.*

13 *For if you live according to the flesh you will die; but if by the Spirit you put to death the deeds of the body, you will live.*

14 *For as many as are led by the Spirit of God, these are sons of God.*

15 *For you did not receive the spirit of bondage again to fear, but you received the Spirit of adoption by whom we cry out, "Abba, Father."*

16 *The Spirit Himself bears witness with our spirit that we are children of God,*

17 *and if children, then heirs—heirs of God and joint heirs with Christ, if indeed we suffer with [Him], that we may also be glorified together.*

18 *For I consider that the sufferings of this present time are not worthy [to be compared] with the glory which shall be revealed in us.*

in the likeness of sinful flesh (v. 3)—Christ was fully man, but without the unredeemed humanness or fleshly nature of sinners.

walk (v. 4)—one's manner of living

set their minds (v. 5)—a basic orientation or disposition of the mind that is set on satisfying the cravings of the flesh

spiritually minded (v. 6)—focused on the things of the Spirit

dwells (v. 9)—makes one's home

put to death the deeds of the body (v. 13)—the ongoing, lifelong process of relying on the Spirit's strength to resist fleshly urges and to carry out God's commands

led by the Spirit (v. 14)—usually by illuminating the Scripture so that our sinful, finite minds can grasp God's will

spirit of bondage . . . to fear (v. 15)—The unredeemed have no lasting peace because of the effects of sin and the prospect of punishment.

bears witness with our spirit (v. 16)—by fruitfulness and power, not mystical voices

heirs (v. 17)—We stand to inherit all that God is and has.

19 For the earnest expectation of the creation eagerly waits for the revealing of the sons of God.

20 For the creation was subjected to futility, not willingly, but because of Him who subjected [it] in hope;

21 because the creation itself also will be delivered from the bondage of corruption into the glorious liberty of the children of God.

22 For we know that the whole creation groans and labors with birth pangs together until now.

23 Not only [that], but we also who have the firstfruits of the Spirit, even we ourselves groan within ourselves, eagerly waiting for the adoption, the redemption of our body.

24 For we were saved in this hope, but hope that is seen is not hope; for why does one still hope for what he sees?

25 But if we hope for what we do not see, we eagerly wait for [it] with perseverance.

26 Likewise the Spirit also helps in our weaknesses. For we do not know what we should pray for as we ought, but the Spirit Himself makes intercession for us with groanings which cannot be uttered.

27 Now He who searches the hearts knows what the mind of the Spirit [is], because He makes intercession for the saints according to [the will of] God.

28 And we know that all things work together for good to those who love God, to those who are the called according to [His] purpose.

29 For whom He foreknew, He also predestined [to be] conformed to the image of His Son, that He might be the firstborn among many brethren.

30 Moreover whom He predestined, these He also called; whom He called, these He also justified; and whom He justified, these He also glorified.

31 What then shall we say to these things? If God [is] for us, who [can be] against us?

32 He who did not spare His own Son, but delivered Him up for us all, how shall He not with Him also freely give us all things?

---

futility (v. 20)—a reference to the effects of the curse (Genesis 3:17–19)

firstfruits of the Spirit (v. 23)—The changes God works in us are evidence of the truth that we will one day be like Christ.

creation eagerly waits . . . groans (vv. 19–22)—the universal longing for the removal of the curse

groanings which cannot be uttered (v. 26)—divine articulations within the Trinity, profound appeals for the welfare of God's people

all things work together for good (v. 28)—Our sovereign God orchestrates every event in life to bring glory to Himself and benefit (temporal or eternal) His children.

foreknew (v. 29)—not omniscience, but the divine choice to set His love on us and establish a relationship with us

predestined (v. 30)—literally, "to mark out," "appoint," or "determine beforehand"

If (v. 31)—since

33 *Who shall bring a charge against God's elect? [It is] God who justifies.*

34 *Who [is] he who condemns? [It is] Christ who died, and furthermore is also risen, who is even at the right hand of God, who also makes intercession for us.*

35 *Who shall separate us from the love of Christ? [Shall] tribulation, or distress, or persecution, or famine, or nakedness, or peril, or sword?*

36 *As it is written: "For Your sake we are killed all day long; We are accounted as sheep for the slaughter."*

37 *Yet in all these things we are more than conquerors through Him who loved us.*

38 *For I am persuaded that neither death nor life, nor angels nor principalities nor powers, nor things present nor things to come,*

39 *nor height nor depth, nor any other created thing, shall be able to separate us from the love of God which is in Christ Jesus our Lord.*

Understanding the Text

2) According to this chapter, what acts/ministries does the Holy Spirit perform in us, through us, and for us?

_____

_____

_____

_____

3) How does the Spirit's presence and work change our very nature?

_____

_____

_____

_____

4) What does Paul mean by the references to "groaning" in this chapter (vv. 22–23)?

_____

_____

_____

Cross-Reference

Consider Christ's promise of the Spirit to His followers, given in the upper room.

John 14:15–17

15 *"If you love Me, keep My commandments.*

16 *"And I will pray the Father, and He will give you another Helper, that He may abide with you forever—*

17 *"the Spirit of truth, whom the world cannot receive, because it neither sees Him nor knows Him; but you know Him, for He dwells with you and will be in you.*

Exploring the Meaning

5) What is the significance that Christ tells his disciples to "keep My commandments" and then immediately promises them the indwelling Spirit of God?

_____

_____

_____

_____

6) Read Galatians 5:22–23. How can the presence of these qualities in a believer's life bring a sense of hope and expectation?

_____

_____

_____

7) Read Colossians 1:28 and 1 John 3:2. What do these verses (and 8:29) say about our destiny? How does the Spirit contribute to this?

_____

_____

_____

Summing Up . . .

"The Spirit-filled life does not come through mystical or ecstatic experiences but from studying and submitting oneself to Scripture. As a believer faithfully and submissively saturates his mind and heart with God's truth, his Spirit-controlled behavior will follow as surely as night follows day. When we are filled with God's truth and led by His Spirit, even our involuntary reactions—those that happen when we don't have time to consciously decide what to do or say—will be godly."—*John MacArthur*

Reflecting on the Text

8) Contrary to much of what is portrayed in religious television programming, the Holy Spirit was not given so that believers could enjoy ecstatic, feel-good experiences. He is not a spiritual narcotic with which we try to numb the pain in our lives. The Spirit lives in us to change us.

The Scottish theologian David Brown, in discussing the command in 8:13 to "put to death the deeds of the body," wrote, "If you don't kill sin, sin will kill you."

How, practically speaking, can God's indwelling Spirit empower you for victory over sin today?

_____

_____

_____

_____

9) On a scale of 1–10, with 1 being "carnal" and 10 being "Christlike," how would you evaluate your "life in the Spirit" right now? What needs to change?

_____

_____

_____

10) Write three words or phrases from this chapter that you intend to meditate upon this week.

_____

_____

_____

Recording Your Thoughts

_____

_____

_____

_____

_____

_____

For further study, see the following passages:

Deuteronomy 8:15–16	Luke 1:6	Luke 22:40, 44–45
John 15:18–21	Acts 1:8	Acts 2:23
Acts 13:38–39	1 Corinthians 2:14–16	1 Corinthians 15:35–44
2 Corinthians 12:13, 27	Galatians 3:10, 21	Ephesians 2:5
Ephesians 4:17	Philippians 1:6	Philippians 3:19
Colossians 3:2, 4, 16	Hebrews 2:14–15, 17–18	Hebrews 4:15
1 Peter 1:4	1 Peter 2:11	1 John 1:7
1 John 4:18		

God's Eternal Plan

Opening Thought

1) Christians and Jews have a long and strange history.

Many professed Christians through the centuries have fanned the flames of anti-Semitism, leading to horrendous persecution of the Jewish people. In recent years, however, many evangelical leaders have been Israel's biggest supporters, siding with them in almost every territorial dispute.

What accounts for this wildly conflicting response over the centuries among Christians to the Jewish people?

_____

_____

_____

_____

_____

_____

_____

_____

_____

_____

Background of the Passage

Romans 9—11 is one of the most fascinating passages in the New Testament, filled with essential and very practical doctrine and focused on Israel, God's chosen people.

Some have argued that these chapters are a parenthetical body of teaching, largely unrelated to the rest of the epistle. Clearly if Paul had left out chapters 9—11, the overall argument and flow of the letter would be unbroken. His beautiful song of praise, hope, and assurance at the end of chapter 8 flows naturally into chapter 12.

This Jewish apostle to the Gentiles, however, wanted to clarify some truths regarding Israel and her people as well as contradict some prevailing false-hoods over which many Christians (especially Jewish believers) were stumbling. Specifically Paul wanted to address the question of whether, in light of Christ's offer of salvation to all Gentiles, the Jews had been forsaken by God as a people. Did they still have a unique place or purpose in God's plan of redemption? Why, if they were God's chosen people, did they so stubbornly reject His Messiah?

With profound wisdom and holy reason, Paul demonstrates that our sovereign God will be faithful to keep all His promises and that Israel still has a future in the purposes of God.

Bible Passage

Read 9:1—11:36, noting the key words and definitions to the right of the passage.

Romans 9:1—11:36

¹ *I tell the truth in Christ, I am not lying, my conscience also bearing me witness in the Holy Spirit,*

² *that I have great sorrow and continual grief in my heart.*

³ *For I could wish that I myself were accursed from Christ for my brethren, my countrymen according to the flesh,*

⁴ *who are Israelites, to whom [pertain] the adoption, the glory, the covenants, the giving of the*

accursed (v. 3)—The Greek word is *anathema*, meaning "to devote to destruction in eternal hell."

glory (v. 4)—the Shekinah, cloud signifying God's presence in the Holy of Holies or among His people

covenants (v. 4)—legally binding agreements or contracts, used

law, the service [of God], and the promises;

5 of whom [are] the fathers and from whom, according to the flesh, Christ [came], who is over all, [the] eternally blessed God. Amen.

6 But it is not that the word of God has taken no effect. For they [are] not all Israel who [are] of Israel,

7 nor [are they] all children because they are the seed of Abraham; but, "In Isaac your seed shall be called."

8 That is, those who [are] the children of the flesh, these [are] not the children of God; but the children of the promise are counted as the seed.

9 For this [is] the word of promise: "At this time I will come and Sarah shall have a son."

10 And not only [this], but when Rebecca also had conceived by one man, [even] by our father Isaac

11 (for [the children] not yet being born, nor having done any good or evil, that the purpose of God according to election might stand, not of works but of Him who calls),

12 it was said to her, "The older shall serve the younger."

13 As it is written, "Jacob I have loved, but Esau I have hated."

14 What shall we say then? [Is there] unrighteousness with God? Certainly not!

15 For He says to Moses, "I will have mercy on whomever I will have mercy, and I will have compassion on whomever I will have compassion."

16 So then [it is] not of him who wills, nor of him who runs, but of God who shows mercy.

17 For the Scripture says to Pharaoh, "For this very purpose I have raised you up, that I may show My power in you, and that My name may be declared in all the earth."

18 Therefore He has mercy on whom He wills, and whom He wills He hardens.

19 You will say to me then, "Why does He still find fault? For who has resisted His will?"

here of the promises between God and His people

fathers (v. 5)—Israel's patriarchs

children of the flesh (v. 8)— Abraham's children through Hagar and Keturah

not of works, but of Him who calls (v. 11)—God chose Jacob before he was and apart from any possible human merit to demonstrate that election is the prerogative of God.

who wills (v. 16)—Salvation is not of human initiative.

20 *But indeed, O man, who are you to reply against God? Will the thing formed say to him who formed [it], "Why have you made me like this?"*

21 *Does not the potter have power over the clay, from the same lump to make one vessel for honor and another for dishonor?*

22 *[What] if God, wanting to show [His] wrath and to make His power known, endured with much longsuffering the vessels of wrath prepared for destruction,*

23 *and that He might make known the riches of His glory on the vessels of mercy, which He had prepared beforehand for glory,*

24 *[even] us whom He called, not of the Jews only, but also of the Gentiles?*

25 *As He says also in Hosea: "I will call them My people, who were not My people, And her beloved, who was not beloved."*

26 *"And it shall come to pass in the place where it was said to them, '[You are] not My people,' There they shall be called sons of the living God."*

27 *Isaiah also cries out concerning Israel: "Though the number of the children of Israel be as the sand of the sea, The remnant will be saved.*

28 *For He will finish the work and cut [it] short in righteousness, Because the LORD will make a short work upon the earth."*

29 *And as Isaiah said before: "Unless the LORD of Sabaoth had left us a seed, We would have become like Sodom, And we would have been made like Gomorrah."*

30 *What shall we say then? That Gentiles, who did not pursue righteousness, have attained to righteousness, even the righteousness of faith;*

31 *but Israel, pursuing the law of righteousness, has not attained to the law of righteousness.*

32 *Why? Because [they did] not [seek it] by faith, but as it were, by the works of the law. For they stumbled at that stumbling stone.*

vessels of wrath (v. 22)—those allowed to incur the just penalty for their sin

Lord of Sabaoth (v. 29)—Lord of hosts or armies, a reference to God's all-encompassing sovereignty

33 As it is written: "Behold, I lay in Zion a stumbling stone and rock of offense, And whoever believes on Him will not be put to shame."

1 Brethren, my heart's desire and prayer to God for Israel is that they may be saved.

2 For I bear them witness that they have a zeal for God, but not according to knowledge.

3 For they being ignorant of God's righteousness, and seeking to establish their own righteousness, have not submitted to the righteousness of God.

4 For Christ [is] the end of the law for righteousness to everyone who believes.

5 For Moses writes about the righteousness which is of the law, "The man who does those things shall live by them."

6 But the righteousness of faith speaks in this way, "Do not say in your heart, 'Who will ascend into heaven?'" (that is, to bring Christ down [from above])

7 or, "Who will descend into the abyss?'" (that is, to bring Christ up from the dead).

8 But what does it say? "The word is near you, in your mouth and in your heart" (that is, the word of faith which we preach):

9 that if you confess with your mouth the Lord Jesus and believe in your heart that God has raised Him from the dead, you will be saved.

10 For with the heart one believes unto righteousness, and with the mouth confession is made unto salvation.

11 For the Scripture says, "Whoever believes on Him will not be put to shame."

12 For there is no distinction between Jew and Greek, for the same Lord over all is rich to all who call upon Him.

13 For "whoever calls on the name of the LORD shall be saved."

14 How then shall they call on Him in whom they have not believed? And how shall they believe in

zeal for God (10:2)—fierce attempts to live out God's law; fervent opposition to Judaism's opponents

Christ is the end of the law (v. 4)—That is, trusting in Christ is the end of the futile quest of trying to fulfill the law in hopes of being seen as righteous in the sight of God.

confession (v. 10)—literally, "to say the same thing," thus to agree with God the Father's declaration that Jesus is Savior and Lord

Him of whom they have not heard? And how shall they hear without a preacher?

15 And how shall they preach unless they are sent? As it is written: "How beautiful are the feet of those who preach the gospel of peace, Who bring glad tidings of good things!"

16 But they have not all obeyed the gospel. For Isaiah says, "Lord, who has believed our report?"

17 So then faith [comes] by hearing, and hearing by the word of God.

18 But I say, have they not heard? Yes indeed: "Their sound has gone out to all the earth, And their words to the ends of the world."

19 But I say, did Israel not know? First Moses says: "I will provoke you to jealousy by [those who are] not a nation, I will move you to anger by a foolish nation."

20 But Isaiah is very bold and says: "I was found by those who did not seek Me; I was made manifest to those who did not ask for Me."

21 But to Israel he says: "All day long I have stretched out My hands To a disobedient and contrary people."

1 I say then, has God cast away His people? Certainly not! For I also am an Israelite, of the seed of Abraham, [of] the tribe of Benjamin.

2 God has not cast away His people whom He foreknew. Or do you not know what the Scripture says of Elijah, how he pleads with God against Israel, saying,

3 "LORD, they have killed Your prophets and torn down Your altars, and I alone am left, and they seek my life"?

4 But what does the divine response say to him? "I have reserved for Myself seven thousand men who have not bowed the knee to Baal."

5 Even so then, at this present time there is a remnant according to the election of grace.

6 And if by grace, then [it is] no longer of works;

the word of God (v. 17)—more accurately, "the word of Christ," that is, the message about Christ, the gospel

cast away (11:1)—to thrust away from one's self

remnant (v. 5)—Though the national leadership had spurned Christ, thousands of individual Jews had believed in Him (Acts 2:41 and 4:4).

otherwise grace is no longer grace. But if [it is] of works, it is no longer grace; otherwise work is no longer work.

7 *What then? Israel has not obtained what it seeks; but the elect have obtained it, and the rest were blinded.*

8 *Just as it is written: "God has given them a spirit of stupor, Eyes that they should not see And ears that they should not hear, To this very day."*

9 *And David says: "Let their table become a snare and a trap, A stumbling block and a recompense to them.*

10 *Let their eyes be darkened, so that they do not see, and bow down their back always."*

11 *I say then, have they stumbled that they should fall? Certainly not! But through their fall, to provoke them to jealousy, salvation [has come] to the Gentiles.*

12 *Now if their fall [is] riches for the world, and their failure riches for the Gentiles, how much more their fullness!*

13 *For I speak to you Gentiles; inasmuch as I am an apostle to the Gentiles, I magnify my ministry,*

14 *if by any means I may provoke to jealousy [those who are] my flesh and save some of them.*

15 *For if their being cast away [is] the reconciling of the world, what [will] their acceptance [be] but life from the dead?*

16 *For if the firstfruit [is] holy, the lump [is] also [holy]; and if the root [is] holy, so [are] the branches.*

17 *And if some of the branches were broken off, and you, being a wild olive tree, were grafted in among them, and with them became a partaker of the root and fatness of the olive tree,*

18 *do not boast against the branches. But if you do boast, [remember that] you do not support the root, but the root supports you.*

19 *You will say then, "Branches were broken off that I might be grafted in."*

20 *Well [said]. Because of unbelief they were broken*

root (v. 16)—the patriarchs Abraham, Isaac, and Jacob

branches (v. 16ff.)—the patriarch's descendants; that is, the nation of Israel

71

off, and you stand by faith. Do not be haughty, but fear.

21 For if God did not spare the natural branches, He may not spare you either.

22 Therefore consider the goodness and severity of God: on those who fell, severity; but toward you, goodness, if you continue in [His] goodness. Otherwise you also will be cut off.

23 And they also, if they do not continue in unbelief, will be grafted in, for God is able to graft them in again.

24 For if you were cut out of the olive tree which is wild by nature, and were grafted contrary to nature into a cultivated olive tree, how much more will these, who [are] natural [branches], be grafted into their own olive tree?

25 For I do not desire, brethren, that you should be ignorant of this mystery, lest you should be wise in your own opinion, that blindness in part has happened to Israel until the fullness of the Gentiles has come in.

26 And so all Israel will be saved, as it is written: "The Deliverer will come out of Zion, And He will turn away ungodliness from Jacob;

27 For this [is] My covenant with them, When I take away their sins."

28 Concerning the gospel [they are] enemies for your sake, but concerning the election [they are] beloved for the sake of the fathers.

29 For the gifts and the calling of God [are] irrevocable.

30 For as you were once disobedient to God, yet have now obtained mercy through their disobedience,

31 even so these also have now been disobedient, that through the mercy shown you they also may obtain mercy.

32 For God has committed them all to disobedience, that He might have mercy on all.

33 Oh, the depth of the riches both of the wisdom and knowledge of God! How unsearchable [are]

goodness and severity (v. 22)—God's attributes are not at odds.

the gifts . . . are irrevocable (v. 29)—God's sovereign election of Israel is unconditional and unchangeable.

God has committed them all to disobedience (v. 32)—God is not the author of sin, but He allows sinful inclinations so that He can receive glory in both mercy and judgment.

His judgments and His ways past finding out!
34 *"For who has known the mind of the LORD? Or who has become His counselor?"*
35 *"Or who has first given to Him And it shall be repaid to him?"*
36 *For of Him and through Him and to Him [are] all things, to whom [be] glory forever. Amen.*

Understanding the Text

2) How does Paul argue in chapter 9 that Israel's unbelief is consistent with God's plan?

_____

_____

_____

_____

3) What agricultural imagery does Paul use in chapter 11 to demonstrate that God's setting aside of Israel is not a permanent condition?

_____

_____

_____

_____

Cross-Reference

Notice how this passage echoes the theme of chapters 9—11 that God is sovereign and can do as He wishes with His creatures (without violating His goodness or mercy).

Jeremiah 18:1–10

1 *The word which came to Jeremiah from the LORD, saying:*
2 *"Arise and go down to the potter's house, and there I will cause you to hear my words."*

³ *Then I went down to the potter's house, and there he was, making something at the wheel.*

⁴ *And the vessel that he made of clay was marred in the hand of the potter; so he made it again into another vessel, as it seemed good to the potter to make.*

⁵ *Then the word of the LORD came to me, saying:*

⁶ *"O house of Israel, can I not do with you as this potter?" says the LORD. "Look, as the clay [is] in the potter's hand, so [are] you in My hand, O house of Israel!*

⁷ *"The instant I speak concerning a nation and concerning a kingdom, to pluck up, to pull down, and to destroy [it],*

⁸ *"if that nation against whom I have spoken turns from its evil, I will relent of the disaster that I thought to bring upon it.*

⁹ *"And the instant I speak concerning a nation and concerning a kingdom, to build and to plant [it],*

¹⁰ *"if it does evil in My sight so that it does not obey My voice, then I will relent concerning the good with which I said I would benefit it.*

Exploring the Meaning

4) Why do the doctrines of divine sovereignty and election make so many people uncomfortable (or even downright angry)?

_____

_____

_____

_____

_____

5) Read Mark 7:1–13. How is it that zealous religiosity can blind people to the truth of the gospel?

_____

_____

_____

_____

6) Read Revelation 7:9–12. What does this suggest about the future relationship between Jews and Gentiles?

_____

_____

_____

_____

Summing Up . . .

"Contrary to what some sincere Christians maintain, God cannot be finished with the nation of Israel—for the obvious reason that all of his promises to her have not yet been fulfilled. If God were through with His chosen nation, His Word would be false and His integrity discredited."—*John MacArthur*

Reflecting on the Text

7) Given what you've seen in these chapters, what should be the modern-day Christian's attitude toward the Jews?

_____

_____

_____

_____

8) Paul's love and concern for his countrymen was such that he wished in agony, that he could trade places with them, literally that he could go to hell so that they might be saved. How does a believer in Christ develop such a compassion for those who are lost?

_____

_____

_____

_____

9) Paul ends his reflection on God's faithfulness and mercy with a magnificent doxology. If you were to write a four sentence tribute of praise to God for including you in his eternal plan of salvation, what would it say?

_____

_____

_____

_____

Recording Your Thoughts

_____

_____

_____

_____

_____

_____

_____

_____

_____

For further study, see the following passages:

Genesis 12:3	Genesis 32:28	Exodus 4:22
Exodus 24:16	Exodus 32:32	Exodus 34:5–7
1 Samuel 12:22	Psalm 7:9	Psalm 48:10
Psalm 104:24	Isaiah 10:22–23	Isaiah 52:7
Jeremiah 9:23–24	Malachi 1:2–3	John 4:22
John 6:37	Acts 18:6	Acts 22:3
Acts 26:4–5	1 Corinthians 1:9	1 Corinthians 8:6
1 Corinthians 12:3	Galatians 3:28–29	1 Thessalonians 2:10
Hebrews 8:7–13	1 Peter 1:3–4	

Opening Thought

1) Many, if not most, modern-day Christians (at least in North America), are a restless lot. They scramble to conferences that promise a fuller, richer, more abundant Christian life. They buy books by the boatload on how to find a closer walk with the Lord. They frantically search for mystical or ecstatic experiences and move among spiritual fads.

As a result, the Church, overall, is weak and powerless, and scoffed at by the world. Few pagans who look on from a distance find much that is attractive.

What is wrong? Why is the Church (and so many individual believers) often such a poor advertisement for the gospel? Why do so many Christians feel unfulfilled?

_____

_____

_____

_____

_____

_____

_____

_____

_____

Background of the Passage

After 11 chapters of rich theological truth, Paul spends the balance of his letter to the Romans explaining how these doctrines should look in a believer's or congregation's daily life. This is a repeated theme in Paul's writings: Theology can *never* be divorced from life; it *always* has practical ramifications and implications.

Paul's description here—what has been called "the normal Christian life"—is nothing short of supernatural! Paul demonstrates that when a believer gives himself or herself fully to God and then, in the power of the Spirit, lives out in experience what is already true of him or her positionally and actually, the result is staggering, mind-boggling. Such an other-worldly life will be like a bright neon sign in a dark culture.

Christians who are living sacrifices in the service of God are godly, not worldly; transformed, not conformed; humble, not proud; helpful and generous, not stingy; unified with others, not divided from them; loving, not hypocritical and hateful; other-centered, not self-absorbed; enthusiastic, not blah; forgiving, not vengeful.

To find out more about this kind of supernatural life, read on.

Bible Passage

Read 12:1–21, noting the key words and definitions to the right of the passage.

Romans 12:1–21

¹ *I beseech you therefore, brethren, by the mercies of God, that you present your bodies a living sacrifice, holy, acceptable to God, [which is] your reasonable service.*

² *And do not be conformed to this world, but be transformed by the renewing of your mind, that you may prove what [is] that good and acceptable and perfect will of God.*

³ *For I say, through the grace given to me, to everyone who is among you, not to think [of himself] more highly than he ought to think, but to think soberly, as God has dealt to each one a measure of faith.*

⁴ *For as we have many members in one body, but*

beseech (v. 1)—urge, admonish, encourage; from the same Greek word that means to call alongside for help

therefore (v. 1)—Since all things were created for the glory of God (11:36), we should live our lives for the same purpose.

mercies of God (v. 1)—a phrase summarizing the gracious, extravagant work of God on behalf of sinners that Paul had discussed in chapters 1—11

present your bodies (v. 1)—Believers are called to devote or offer themselves completely and

all the members do not have the same function,

5 so we, [being] many, are one body in Christ, and individually members of one another.

6 Having then gifts differing according to the grace that is given to us, [let us use them]: if prophecy, [let us prophesy] in proportion to our faith;

7 or ministry, [let us use it] in [our] ministering; he who teaches, in teaching;

8 he who exhorts, in exhortation; he who gives, with liberality; he who leads, with diligence; he who shows mercy, with cheerfulness.

9 [Let] love [be] without hypocrisy. Abhor what is evil. Cling to what is good.

10 [Be] kindly affectionate to one another with brotherly love, in honor giving preference to one another;

11 not lagging in diligence, fervent in spirit, serving the Lord;

12 rejoicing in hope, patient in tribulation, continuing steadfastly in prayer;

13 distributing to the needs of the saints, given to hospitality.

14 Bless those who persecute you; bless and do not curse.

15 Rejoice with those who rejoice, and weep with those who weep.

16 Be of the same mind toward one another. Do not set your mind on high things, but associate with the humble. Do not be wise in your own opinion.

17 Repay no one evil for evil. Have regard for good things in the sight of all men.

18 If it is possible, as much as depends on you, live peaceably with all men.

19 Beloved, do not avenge yourselves, but [rather] give place to wrath; for it is written, "Vengeance [is] Mine, I will repay," says the Lord.

20 Therefore "If your enemy is hungry, feed him; If he is thirsty, give him a drink; For in so doing you will heap coals of fire on his head."

21 Do not be overcome by evil, but overcome evil with good.

unreservedly to the Lord. This is the only way we can honor God with our unredeemed bodies.

reasonable service (v. 1)—Reasonable means logical; in light of all God has done for us, this is what we should do for Him.

conformed (v. 2)—to assume an external appearance that does not match the internal reality

this world (v. 2)—literally, "this age"; the system of beliefs and values that comprise the spirit of the times in which we live

transformed (v. 2)—The Greek term is the source of the English term "metamorphosis"; the meaning is to change in appearance (because of the inner changes that have and are taking place).

renewing of your mind (v. 2)—to be made new in the way one thinks by being saturated with the Word of God and controlled by the Spirit of God

soberly (v. 3)—the exercise of sound judgment

measure of faith (v. 3)—the correct proportion of the spiritual gift needed to fulfill one's role in the body of Christ

many members . . . one body (v. 4)—The Church is a unified diversity.

prophecy (v. 6)—literally, "speaking forth" the truth of God, not necessarily predicting the future

ministry (v. 7)—service, from the Greek word from which we get our word "deacon"

teaching (v. 7)—the ability to interpret, clarify, systematize, and explain God's truth clearly

liberality (v. 8)—simplicity, single-mindedness, and openhearted generosity

leads (v. 8)—literally, "standing before"

in honor giving preference (v. 10)—showing genuine appreciation and admiration for fellow believers by putting them first

fervent in spirit (v. 11)—literally, "to boil in spirit," that is, to have an inner enthusiasm that results in productive labor

given to hospitality (v. 13)—Literally "pursuing the love of strangers," this kind of openness and generosity should be the hallmark of believers.

Repay no one evil for evil (v. 17)—a ban on individual application of the "eye for an eye" principle of justice

heap coals of fire on his head (v. 20)—a reference to an Egyptian custom of demonstrating shame and contrition by carrying a pan of burning coals on one's head; kindness to hateful, undeserving enemies produces shame

Understanding the Text

2) Paul begins chapter 12 with a call for believers, in view of all that God has given them, to give themselves fully and completely—body, mind, and will—to God. According to Paul, what is involved in doing this?

_____

_____

_____

_____

3) What in chapter 12 proves that the Christian life is not designed to be lived out in isolation?

_____

_____

_____

_____

_____

4) Some skeptics see Paul's list of commands in chapter 12 as nothing more than a New Testament version of the Old Testament law. If keeping God's law is impossible (as Paul has already argued in this letter), how can believers in the Church expect to live out all these "dos and don'ts"?

_____

_____

_____

_____

_____

Cross-Reference

Read 1 Peter 4:7–11 and note the kind of living described.

7 But the end of all things is at hand; therefore be serious and watchful in your prayers.
8 And above all things have fervent love for one another, for "love will cover a multitude of sins."
9 [Be] hospitable to one another without grumbling.
10 As each one has received a gift, minister it to one another, as good stewards of the manifold grace of God.
11 If anyone speaks, [let him speak] as the oracles of God. If anyone ministers, [let him do it] as with the ability which God supplies, that in all things God may be glorified through Jesus Christ, to whom belong the glory and the dominion forever and ever. Amen.

Exploring the Meaning

5) What insights does Peter add to the doctrine of spiritual gifts presented in chapter 12? Who has the gifts and what is their purpose?

_____

_____

_____

_____

_____

(passages to consider: 1 Corinthians 12; Ephesians 4)

6) According to Paul, what attitudes and actions glorify God and build up the body? What attitudes and actions dishonor God and tear down the body of Christ?

_____

_____

_____

_____

_____

7) What happens in a human body when certain parts or organs stop working (whether by sickness or rebellion)? What is the parallel here to the body of Christ?

_____

_____

_____

_____

Summing Up . . .

"Supernatural living is conforming our outer lives to our inner lives, living out the redeemed, purified, and holy nature we have in Jesus Christ, becoming in practice what we are in position and new creation.

"But supernatural living is not a mystical, undefined life based on elusive good impulses and sincere intentions. It is practical living that results from conscious obedience to God's standards of righteousness, a life lived within divinely-ordained parameters. It is thinking, speaking, and acting in daily conformity with God's Word and will."—*John MacArthur*

Reflecting on the Text

8) The nineteenth-century Englishman Robert C. Chapman wrote, "Seeing that so many preach Christ and so few live Christ, I will aim to live Him." What principle or truth in this lesson do you need to stop talking about and start living?

_____

_____

_____

_____

_____

9) Based on your experiences and the evaluations of Christian leaders and friends, what are your spiritual gifts? How are you using these God-given abilities to serve the body of Christ?

_____

_____

_____

_____

_____

_____

10) Write out a verse from chapter 12 that you will memorize and meditate upon this week:

_____

_____

_____

_____

_____

Recording Your Thoughts

_____

_____

_____

_____

_____

_____

_____

_____

_____

_____

_____

_____

_____

_____

_____

For further study, see the following passages:

Deuteronomy 19:21	Proverbs 14:21, 31	Proverbs 25:21–22
Matthew 17:2	Acts 18:24, 25	Acts 20:35
1 Corinthians 12:7, 11	2 Corinthians 3:18	2 Corinthians 4:4
2 Corinthians 8:2–5	Galatians 2:9	Ephesians 1:3–14
Philippians 2:3	Philippians 4:8	Colossians 1:28
1 Thessalonians 4:9	1 Thessalonians 5:17	2 Timothy 4:2
Hebrews 2:3–4	Hebrews 9:11–12	James 5:11
1 Peter 2:21–23	Jude 3	

Real to Reel

Opening Thought

1) Consider these actual activities by so-called "Christians":
   - "Anti-government" extremists who refuse to pay taxes
   - Vigilantes who assassinate abortion doctors
   - Fringe groups that form their own "sovereign nations" within the boundaries of the United States
   - Pastors who pray publicly for the death of the President or Supreme Court justices
   - Congregations that express glee over the deaths of homosexuals to AIDS
   - Churches that accept and sanction homosexual marriages, heterosexual immorality, and divorce for any reason

What effect do these behaviors have on those in the government and in culture who already view the Church and Christians with suspicion or scorn?

_____

_____

_____

_____

_____

_____

_____

_____

_____

Background of the Passage

The first eleven chapters of this epistle (in particular chapters 1—8) explain in marvelous detail what it means to be saved and how people become saved—by being justified by God's grace working through faith.

This monumental miracle of salvation impacts every relationship of the believer. Paul upholds these implications as chapter 12 begins. First, and most important and obvious, is the effect on one's relationship to God. When we are saved, our initial response should be to fully present our "bodies a living sacrifice, holy, acceptable to God, which is [our] spiritual service of worship" (12:1). The apostle's next concern is for having right relationships in the church with brothers and sisters in Christ (12:3–16) and even with enemies (vv. 17–21).

After dealing with these matters, the inspired apostle focuses chapter 13 on the need to have right relationships in the world. First, we must be subject to, demonstrate respect for, and pay taxes to the governing authorities. Secondly, we must love our neighbors and live holy lives that stand out against the dark backdrop of a world without God.

Bible Passage

Read 13:1–14, noting the key words and definitions to the right of the passage.

Romans 13:1–14

¹ *Let every soul be subject to the governing authorities. For there is no authority except from God, and the authorities that exist are appointed by God.*

² *Therefore whoever resists the authority resists the ordinance of God, and those who resist will bring judgment on themselves.*

³ *For rulers are not a terror to good works, but to evil. Do you want to be unafraid of the authority? Do what is good, and you will have praise from the same.*

⁴ *For he is God's minister to you for good. But if you do evil, be afraid; for he does not bear the*

be subject (v. 1)—used elsewhere of a soldier's absolute obedience to his superior officer

no authority except from God (v. 1)—As the Sovereign of the universe, God established the various authority structures (government, family, church, employer).

resists the ordinance of God (v. 2)—To disobey the government is to disregard that which has been ordained of God.

judgment (v. 2)—temporal, at the hands of the human authorities

sword in vain; for he is God's minister, an avenger to [execute] wrath on him who practices evil.

5 Therefore [you] must be subject, not only because of wrath but also for conscience' sake.

6 For because of this you also pay taxes, for they are God's ministers attending continually to this very thing.

7 Render therefore to all their due: taxes to whom taxes [are due], customs to whom customs, fear to whom fear, honor to whom honor.

8 Owe no one anything except to love one another, for he who loves another has fulfilled the law.

9 For the commandments, "You shall not commit adultery," "You shall not murder," "You shall not steal," "You shall not bear false witness," "You shall not covet," and if [there is] any other commandment, are [all] summed up in this saying, namely, "You shall love your neighbor as yourself."

10 Love does no harm to a neighbor; therefore love [is] the fulfillment of the law.

11 And [do] this, knowing the time, that now [it is] high time to awake out of sleep; for now our salvation [is] nearer than when we [first] believed.

12 The night is far spent, the day is at hand. Therefore let us cast off the works of darkness, and let us put on the armor of light.

13 Let us walk properly, as in the day, not in revelry and drunkenness, not in lewdness and lust, not in strife and envy.

14 But put on the Lord Jesus Christ, and make no provision for the flesh, to [fulfill its] lusts.

Do what is good . . . have praise (v. 3)—Law-abiding citizens do not normally need to fear punishment.

God's minister . . . for good (v. 4)—to restrain evil and promote domestic peace

bear the sword (v. 4)—Government has a divine right to execute justice on lawbreakers, even capital punishment.

taxes (v. 6)—The Greek word refers to tribute paid by individuals of occupied nations to their conquerors, an especially odious obligation.

Render (v. 7)—A Greek word signifying the payment of something owed, not a voluntary contribution, but something due.

customs (v. 7)—tolls or taxes on goods

Owe no one anything (v. 8)—not a prohibition against borrowing altogether, but an exhortation to pay debts in a timely fashion

love one another (v. 8)—non-Christians as well as fellow believers

sleep (v. 11)—spiritual lethargy and apathy; non-responsiveness to the things of God

our salvation is nearer (v. 11)—Not the element of justification (a present possession), but the time of our glorification; that is, Christ is coming back.

cast off (v. 12)—an exhortation to repent and get rid of sins

revelry (v. 13)—wild parties, sexual orgies, brawls, riots

make no provision (v. 14)—Do not plan ahead or give forethought to sin.

Understanding the Text

2) What are the God-ordained consequences of defying government authority?

_____

_____

_____

3) How does Paul use four of the Ten Commandments to demonstrate that love is the fulfillment of the law?

_____

_____

_____

_____

4) What facts does Paul use to motivate the believers in Rome to forsake sin and live righteously?

_____

_____

_____

Cross-Reference

Consider how Shadrach, Meshach, and Abed-Nego handled a very public, very difficult situation involving submission to a pagan king's sinful edict.

Daniel 3:12–30

12 "There are certain Jews whom you have set over the affairs of the province of Babylon: Shadrach, Meshach, and Abed-Nego; these men, O king, have not paid due regard to you. They do not serve your gods or worship the gold image which you have set up."

13 Then Nebuchadnezzar, in rage and fury, gave the command to bring Shadrach, Meshach, and Abed-Nego. So they brought these men before the king.

14 Nebuchadnezzar spoke, saying to them, "[Is it] true, Shadrach, Meshach, and Abed-Nego, [that] you do not serve my gods or worship the gold image which I have set up?

15 "Now if you are ready at the time you hear the sound of the horn, flute, harp, lyre, [and] psaltery, in symphony with all kinds of music, and you fall down and worship the image which I have made, [good]! But if you do not worship, you shall be cast immediately into the midst of a burning fiery furnace. And who [is] the god who will deliver you from my hands?"

16 Shadrach, Meshach, and Abed-Nego answered and said to the king, "O Nebuchadnezzar, we have no need to answer you in this matter.

17 "If that [is the case], our God whom we serve is able to deliver us from the burning fiery furnace, and He will deliver [us] from your hand, O king.

18 "But if not, let it be known to you, O king, that we do not serve your gods, nor will we worship the gold image which you have set up."

19 Then Nebuchadnezzar was full of fury, and the expression on his face changed toward Shadrach, Meshach, and Abed-Nego. He spoke and commanded that they heat the furnace seven times more than it was usually heated.

20 And he commanded certain mighty men of valor who [were] in his army to bind Shadrach, Meshach, and Abed-Nego, [and] cast [them] into the burning fiery furnace.

21 Then these men were bound in their coats, their trousers, their turbans, and their [other] garments, and were cast into the midst of the burning fiery furnace.

22 Therefore, because the king's command was urgent, and the furnace exceedingly hot, the flame of the fire killed those men who took up Shadrach, Meshach, and Abed-Nego.

23 And these three men, Shadrach, Meshach, and Abed-Nego, fell down bound into the midst of the burning fiery furnace.

24 Then King Nebuchadnezzar was astonished; and he rose in haste [and] spoke, saying to his counselors, "Did we not cast three men bound into the midst of the fire?" They answered and said to the king, "True, O king."

25 "Look!" he answered, "I see four men loose, walking in the midst of the fire; and they are not hurt, and the form of the fourth is like the Son of God."

26 Then Nebuchadnezzar went near the mouth of the burning fiery furnace [and] spoke, saying, "Shadrach, Meshach, and Abed-Nego, servants of the Most High God, come out, and come [here]." Then Shadrach, Meshach, and Abed-Nego came from the midst of the fire.

27 And the satraps, administrators, governors, and the king's counselors gathered together, and they saw these men on whose bodies the fire had no power; the hair of their head was not singed nor were their garments affected, and the smell of fire was not on them.

28 *Nebuchadnezzar spoke, saying, "Blessed be the God of Shadrach, Meshach, and Abed-Nego, who sent His Angel and delivered His servants who trusted in Him, and they have frustrated the king's word, and yielded their bodies, that they should not serve nor worship any god except their own God!*

29 *"Therefore I make a decree that any people, nation, or language which speaks anything amiss against the God of Shadrach, Meshach, and Abed-Nego shall be cut in pieces, and their houses shall be made an ash heap; because there is no other God who can deliver like this."*

30 *Then the king promoted Shadrach, Meshach, and Abed-Nego in the province of Babylon.*

Exploring the Meaning

5) How did the noble, public behavior of these three God-fearing Jews enhance God's reputation?

_____

_____

_____

_____

6) Read Acts 5:28–29. What exception, if any, is there to the divine command to "be subject to the governing authorities" (v. 1)?

_____

_____

_____

_____

7) What does it mean to "put on the Lord Jesus Christ" (13:14)?

_____

_____

_____

_____

Summing Up . . .

"Believers are to be model citizens, known as law abiding, not rabble-rousing, obedient rather than rebellious, respectful of government rather than demeaning of it. We must speak against sin, against injustice, against immorality and ungodliness with fearful dedication, but we must do it within the framework of civil law and with respect for civil authorities. We are to be a godly society, doing good and living peaceably within an ungodly society, manifesting our transformed lives so that the saving power of God is seen clearly."—*John MacArthur*

Reflecting on the Text

8) What happens to the message of the gospel and the reputation of God and His people, when Christians are belligerent and disrespectful in the public sector?

_____

_____

_____

_____

9) When you consider your current set of elected officials (federal, state, and local), is it easy for you to want to subject yourself to their authority? Do you resent paying taxes to the current administration? Why or why not?

What if an official is corrupt, unlikable, or disreputable? What are our options as believers?

_____

_____

_____

_____

_____

10) Write down the names of three government officials for whom you can pray this week. Take the time to write them each a note expressing your support and gratitude.

_____

_____

_____

_____

Recording Your Thoughts

_____

_____

_____

_____

_____

_____

_____

_____

_____

_____

For further study, see the following passages:

Genesis 9:6	Exodus 1:17	Exodus 22:25
Matthew 5:42	Matthew 22:17–21	Acts 4:19–20
Galatians 4:19	Galatians 5:21	Galatians 6:10
Philippians 3:13–14	1 Timothy 5:16	Titus 3:1–2
Hebrews 10:24–25	1 Peter 2:1	2 Peter 3:14

The Strong & The Weak

Opening Thought

A story:

First Church is having some problems. One group of long-time members doesn't like the young, new pastor. His preaching style is informal (he sometimes doesn't wear a coat and tie!), and he is downplaying (sometimes even ignoring) lots of the old, beloved traditions. He seems to be less enthusiastic about Sunday school than he is about the new, so-called "support and recovery groups."

Meanwhile newcomers to the church love the more contemporary worship (drums and guitars) service and the preacher's storytelling style. Lots of these folks are divorced, and some of them even smoke in the church courtyard between services.

1) Who's right and who's wrong? Is this a healthy congregation? Why or why not?

_____

_____

_____

2) How can a church full of people with different backgrounds, genes, personality types, ways of communicating and thinking, struggles, emotions, values, desires, experiences, expectations, and convictions *ever* expect to find unity?

_____

_____

_____

Background of the Passage

A major theme of the New Testament is that of sin's power to destroy the spiritual and moral character of the church. But outright, blatant sin is not the only danger to a church's spiritual health and unity. Certain attitudes and behavior can destroy fellowship and fruitfulness, and they have crippled the work, the witness, and the unity of countless congregations throughout church history. These problems are caused by differences between Christians over matters that are neither commanded nor forbidden in Scripture. They are matters of personal preference and historic tradition, which, when imposed on others, inevitably cause confusion, strife, ill will, abused consciences, and disharmony.

The particular danger to unity that Paul addresses in 14:1—15:13 is the conflict that easily arises between those to whom he refers as "strong" and "weak" believers, those who are mature in the faith and those who are immature, those who understand and enjoy freedom in Christ and those who still feel either shackled or threatened by certain religious and cultural taboos and practices that were deeply ingrained parts of their lives before coming to Christ.

This section is extremely helpful to anyone who finds himself or herself in a congregation of diverse believers and who struggles to accept those who are different. And isn't that all of us?

Bible Passage

Read 14:1—15:13, noting the key words and definitions to the right of the passage.

Romans 14:1—15:13

¹ *Receive one who is weak in the faith, [but] not to disputes over doubtful things.*

² *For one believes he may eat all things, but he who is weak eats [only] vegetables.*

³ *Let not him who eats despise him who does not eat, and let not him who does not eat judge him who eats; for God has received him.*

weak in faith (v. 1)—a reference to believers' inability to let go of the religious ceremonies and rituals of the past

only vegetables (v. 2)—the strict diet of conscience-stricken Jewish and Gentile believers who could not bring themselves to eat meat that had been sacrificed to idols

4 *Who are you to judge another's servant? To his own master he stands or falls. Indeed, he will be made to stand, for God is able to make him stand.*

5 *One person esteems [one] day above another; another esteems every day [alike]. Let each be fully convinced in his own mind.*

6 *He who observes the day, observes [it] to the Lord; and he who does not observe the day, to the Lord he does not observe [it]. He who eats, eats to the Lord, for he gives God thanks; and he who does not eat, to the Lord he does not eat, and gives God thanks.*

7 *For none of us lives to himself, and no one dies to himself.*

8 *For if we live, we live to the Lord; and if we die, we die to the Lord. Therefore, whether we live or die, we are the Lord's.*

9 *For to this end Christ died and rose and lived again, that He might be Lord of both the dead and the living.*

10 *But why do you judge your brother? Or why do you show contempt for your brother? For we shall all stand before the judgment seat of Christ.*

11 *For it is written: "[As] I live, says the LORD, Every knee shall bow to Me, And every tongue shall confess to God."*

12 *So then each of us shall give account of himself to God.*

13 *Therefore let us not judge one another anymore, but rather resolve this, not to put a stumbling block or a cause to fall in [our] brother's way.*

14 *I know and am convinced by the Lord Jesus that [there is] nothing unclean of itself; but to him who considers anything to be unclean, to him [it is] unclean.*

15 *Yet if your brother is grieved because of [your] food, you are no longer walking in love. Do not destroy with your food the one for whom Christ died.*

---

despise (v. 3)—to have contempt or disdain

judge (v. 3)—to condemn

To his own master he stands or falls (v. 4)—Christ is the ultimate judge of our motives and actions.

Let each be fully convinced (v. 5)—In matters not dictated by Scripture, believers must follow their Spirit-led conscience (regardless of what others say or do).

to the Lord (v. 6)—Whether weak or strong in conscience, our decision must be with a view to bring honor and pleasure to God.

judgment seat of Christ (v. 10)—a future day of accounting before God's throne in which our decisions as believers will be examined

stumbling block (v. 13)—anything a believer does—even biblically permissible things—that causes another to sin

grieved (v. 15)—to cause pain or distress; that is, a weak believer seeing a stronger believer enjoy a freedom that the weak believer is convinced is sin

destroy (v. 15)—in this context, not damnation, but devastation

16 *Therefore do not let your good be spoken of as evil;*

17 *for the kingdom of God is not eating and drinking, but righteousness and peace and joy in the Holy Spirit.*

18 *For he who serves Christ in these things [is] acceptable to God and approved by men.*

19 *Therefore let us pursue the things [which make] for peace and the things by which one may edify another.*

20 *Do not destroy the work of God for the sake of food. All things indeed [are] pure, but [it is] evil for the man who eats with offense.*

21 *[It is] good neither to eat meat nor drink wine nor [do anything] by which your brother stumbles or is offended or is made weak.*

22 *Do you have faith? Have [it] to yourself before God. Happy [is] he who does not condemn himself in what he approves.*

23 *But he who doubts is condemned if he eats, because [he does] not [eat] from faith; for whatever [is] not from faith is sin.*

1 *We then who are strong ought to bear with the scruples of the weak, and not to please ourselves.*

2 *Let each of us please [his] neighbor for [his] good, leading to edification.*

3 *For even Christ did not please Himself; but as it is written, "The reproaches of those who reproached You fell on Me."*

4 *For whatever things were written before were written for our learning, that we through the patience and comfort of the Scriptures might have hope.*

5 *Now may the God of patience and comfort grant you to be like-minded toward one another, according to Christ Jesus,*

6 *that you may with one mind [and] one mouth glorify the God and Father of our Lord Jesus Christ.*

7 *Therefore receive one another, just as Christ also received us, to the glory of God.*

---

your good (v. 16)—one's rightful exercise of Christian liberty

eating and drinking (v. 17)—trivial, nonessentials

approved by men (v. 18)—suggests approval after careful examination; here, it suggests that our righteous behavior and love for one another would be seen as genuine by a skeptical world

bear (15:1)—literally, "to pick up and carry a weight"; the strong believer is to not just tolerate the weaker brother, but is to show consideration and love by shouldering their burdens

Christ did not please Himself (v. 3)—Christ's goal was always to please the Father.

written before (v. 4)—the Old Testament scriptures

receive (v. 7)—to warmly accept and embrace, even with differences

8 *Now I say that Jesus Christ has become a servant to the circumcision for the truth of God, to confirm the promises [made] to the fathers,*

9 *and that the Gentiles might glorify God for [His] mercy, as it is written: "For this reason I will confess to You among the Gentiles, And sing to Your name."*

10 *And again he says: "Rejoice, O Gentiles, with His people!"*

11 *And again: "Praise the LORD, all you Gentiles! Laud Him, all you peoples!"*

12 *And again, Isaiah says: "There shall be a root of Jesse; And He who shall rise to reign over the Gentiles, In Him the Gentiles shall hope."*

13 *Now may the God of hope fill you with all joy and peace in believing, that you may abound in hope by the power of the Holy Spirit.*

the promises made to the fathers, and . . . the Gentiles (vv. 8–9)—God's plan has always been to bring both Jews and Gentiles into His kingdom.

Understanding the Text

3) Why was there so much judging in the Roman church? What was the situation as described by Paul?

_____

_____

_____

_____

4) In areas where the Scripture neither prescribes nor prohibits behavior, what counsel does Paul give for determining a course of action?

_____

_____

_____

_____

_____

5) Behind all the different convictions and possible behaviors, what does Paul suggest should be our ultimate goals when we confront issues not addressed by the Word of God?

_____

_____

_____

_____

Cross-Reference

The Roman church wasn't the only congregation in Paul's time that suffered tension due to differences in the body. Consider the apostle's instruction to the church at Corinth.

1 Corinthians 8:1–13

¹ *Now concerning things offered to idols: We know that we all have knowledge. Knowledge puffs up, but love edifies.*

² *And if anyone thinks that he knows anything, he knows nothing yet as he ought to know.*

³ *But if anyone loves God, this one is known by Him.*

⁴ *Therefore concerning the eating of things offered to idols, we know that an idol [is] nothing in the world, and that [there is] no other God but one.*

⁵ *For even if there are so-called gods, whether in heaven or on earth (as there are many gods and many lords),*

⁶ *yet for us [there is] one God, the Father, of whom [are] all things, and we for Him; and one Lord Jesus Christ, through whom [are] all things, and through whom we [live].*

⁷ *However, [there is] not in everyone that knowledge; for some, with consciousness of the idol, until now eat [it] as a thing offered to an idol; and their conscience, being weak, is defiled.*

⁸ *But food does not commend us to God; for neither if we eat are we the better, nor if we do not eat are we the worse.*

⁹ *But beware lest somehow this liberty of yours become a stumbling block to those who are weak.*

¹⁰ *For if anyone sees you who have knowledge eating in an idol's temple, will not the conscience of him who is weak be emboldened to eat those things offered to idols?*

¹¹ *And because of your knowledge shall the weak brother perish, for whom Christ died?*

¹² *But when you thus sin against the brethren, and wound their weak conscience, you sin against Christ.*

¹³ *Therefore, if food makes my brother stumble, I will never again eat meat, lest I make my brother stumble.*

Exploring the Meaning

6) The struggle in the church at Corinth was over meat that had been sacrificed to idols and then was sold in the nearby marketplace. "Should a Christian eat such meat or not?"—this was the big debate. Some concluded that the meat was fine since idols are manmade and not truly divine. Others could not, in good conscience, enter into this practice. What was Paul's solution?

_____

_____

_____

_____

7) Read Galatians 5:13. We are free in Christ, but for what purpose does Paul say our freedom is to be used?

_____

_____

_____

8) Consider the Twelve Jesus chose to be his closest followers (Mark 3:13–19). We know from the biblical record that these men were from a wide range of backgrounds, political persuasions, and occupations. How does the forming of this diverse group serve as a model for the kind of unity that modern-day congregations can enjoy?

_____

_____

Summing Up . . .

"To accept one another, just as Christ also accepted us, is a sure mark of godliness, and failure to do so is just as surely a mark of carnality. Failure to accept one another in love and compassion is an affront to the Savior who accepted us. A congregation that is divisive, quarrelsome, contentious, and judgmental gives the world reason to ridicule Christ's church and to reject the One who is their only hope of salvation."—*John MacArthur*

Reflecting on the Text

9) What biblical command or principle from this passage is most helpful to you as you think about relating to others in your local church?

_____

_____

_____

_____

10) When dealing with differences between people, four things are necessary: *recognizing* the differences; *working to understand* the differences; *learning to appreciate* the differences; and *wisely utilizing* the differences.

Which of these steps do you have the most difficulty with and why?

_____

_____

_____

_____

11) Write out a short prayer in which you express back to God what you've learned from this lesson.

_____

_____

_____

_____

Recording Your Thoughts

_____

_____

_____

_____

_____

_____

_____

_____

_____

_____

_____

_____

For further study, see the following passages:

Psalm 18:49	Psalm 119:81, 114	Matthew 10:28
John 8:25, 27–29	Acts 10:14–15	1 Corinthians 3:13–15
1 Corinthians 6:9	1 Corinthians 10:23–32	2 Corinthians 5:9–10
Galatians 4:9–10	Galatians 5:22–23	Ephesians 4:32—5:2
Philippians 2:11, 15	Titus 1:15	1 Peter 1:3

Additional Notes

Ministering Together

Opening Thought

1) In most churches, the so-called 80–20 principle is in effect. If you are unfamiliar with this principle, it is the remarkably accurate axiom that 80 percent of the average congregation does only 20 percent of the serving and giving that takes place in the church. Sadly, in most churches, it's the minority (the 20 percent) that is doing the lion's share in terms of work and financial support.

What are the short-term and long-term implications of this for a body of believers? What happens in the hearts of those who are not actively contributing to the ministry? What can happen to those who are working tirelessly?

_____

_____

_____

_____

_____

_____

_____

_____

_____

_____

_____

Background of the Passage

After completing the major doctrinal treatise of this letter (1:18—15:13), Paul now begins what amounts to an epilogue, which comprises comments about his ministry (15:14–21), his plans for future service (15:22–33), personal greetings from himself and others (16:1–24), and a closing benediction (16:25–27).

Because Paul had spoken so forcefully on so many issues to a church he did not found and had never visited, he wants to make sure he does not seem insensitive, presumptuous, or unloving. So Paul makes several important statements in the last paragraphs of his letter—

He commends them corporately for their involvement in the gospel.

He shares a bit of information about his own ministry and future plans.

He reiterates his heart's desire to minister in Rome and to fellowship with the church there.

He mentions by name more than two dozen colleagues and co-workers.

Here, in chapter 16, we get a rare glimpse into Paul's working relationships and close friendships. In this extended passage we sense the deep affection that Paul had for those with whom and to whom he ministered. We also get to see the sincere gratitude the apostle felt for those who had been such a help and encouragement to him in life and ministry.

As the faces of redeemed and transformed Jews and Gentiles flashed through Paul's mind, the apostle closed his epistle, fittingly, with a final hymn of praise: "to God, alone wise, be glory through Jesus Christ forever. Amen" (16:27).

Bible Passage

Read 15:14—16:27, noting the key words and definitions to the right of the passage.

Romans 15:14—16:27

14 *Now I myself am confident concerning you, my brethren, that you also are full of goodness, filled with all knowledge, able also to admonish one another.*

15 *Nevertheless, brethren, I have written more boldly to you on [some] points, as reminding you,*

knowledge (v. 14)—deep, intimate knowledge; doctrinal soundness

admonish (v. 14)—encourage, warn, advise; that is, a comprehensive term for counseling

because of the grace given to me by God,

16 that I might be a minister of Jesus Christ to the Gentiles, ministering the gospel of God, that the offering of the Gentiles might be acceptable, sanctified by the Holy Spirit.

17 Therefore I have reason to glory in Christ Jesus in the things [which pertain] to God.

18 For I will not dare to speak of any of those things which Christ has not accomplished through me, in word and deed, to make the Gentiles obedient—

19 in mighty signs and wonders, by the power of the Spirit of God, so that from Jerusalem and round about to Illyricum I have fully preached the gospel of Christ.

20 And so I have made it my aim to preach the gospel, not where Christ was named, lest I should build on another man's foundation,

21 but as it is written: "To whom He was not announced, they shall see; And those who have not heard shall understand."

22 For this reason I also have been much hindered from coming to you.

23 But now no longer having a place in these parts, and having a great desire these many years to come to you,

24 whenever I journey to Spain, I shall come to you. For I hope to see you on my journey, and to be helped on my way there by you, if first I may enjoy your [company] for a while.

25 But now I am going to Jerusalem to minister to the saints.

26 For it pleased those from Macedonia and Achaia to make a certain contribution for the poor among the saints who are in Jerusalem.

27 It pleased them indeed, and they are their debtors. For if the Gentiles have been partakers of their spiritual things, their duty is also to minister to them in material things.

28 Therefore, when I have performed this and have

minister (v. 16)—one who serves God in some form of public worship

glory (v. 17)—boast; Paul never boasted of his accomplishments, only of what Christ had done through him

signs and wonders (v. 19)—miracles that authenticated true teaching and preaching

another man's foundation (v. 20)—As one with the gift of evangelism, Paul's goal and desire was to minister to those who had never heard.

hindered from coming (v. 22)—an ongoing, providential prevention from getting to Rome

helped on my way (v. 24)—Paul's tactful way of requesting assistance in his proposed evangelistic campaign to Spain

contribution (v. 26)—The Greek word indicates sharing and is usually translated "fellowship" or "communion;" that is, minister and financial supporters are partners.

sealed to them this fruit, I shall go by way of you to Spain.

29 But I know that when I come to you, I shall come in the fullness of the blessing of the gospel of Christ.

30 Now I beg you, brethren, through the Lord Jesus Christ, and through the love of the Spirit, that you strive together with me in prayers to God for me,

31 that I may be delivered from those in Judea who do not believe, and that my service for Jerusalem may be acceptable to the saints,

32 that I may come to you with joy by the will of God, and may be refreshed together with you.

33 Now the God of peace [be] with you all. Amen.

1 I commend to you Phoebe our sister, who is a servant of the church in Cenchrea,

2 that you may receive her in the Lord in a manner worthy of the saints, and assist her in whatever business she has need of you; for indeed she has been a helper of many and of myself also.

3 Greet Priscilla and Aquila, my fellow workers in Christ Jesus,

4 who risked their own necks for my life, to whom not only I give thanks, but also all the churches of the Gentiles.

5 Likewise [greet] the church that is in their house. Greet my beloved Epaenetus, who is the firstfruits of Achaia to Christ.

6 Greet Mary, who labored much for us.

7 Greet Andronicus and Junia, my countrymen and my fellow prisoners, who are of note among the apostles, who also were in Christ before me.

8 Greet Amplias, my beloved in the Lord.

9 Greet Urbanus, our fellow worker in Christ, and Stachys, my beloved.

10 Greet Apelles, approved in Christ. Greet those who are of the [household] of Aristobulus.

11 Greet Herodion, my countryman. Greet those who are of the [household] of Narcissus who are in the Lord.

servant (16:1)—the term from which we get "deacon" and "deaconness"; whether this was an official role is unclear

labored (v. 6)—suggests hard work to the point of exhaustion

12 *Greet Tryphena and Tryphosa, who have labored in the Lord. Greet the beloved Persis, who labored much in the Lord.*

13 *Greet Rufus, chosen in the Lord, and his mother and mine.*

14 *Greet Asyncritus, Phlegon, Hermas, Patrobas, Hermes, and the brethren who are with them.*

15 *Greet Philologus and Julia, Nereus and his sister, and Olympas, and all the saints who are with them.*

16 *Greet one another with a holy kiss. The churches of Christ greet you.*

17 *Now I urge you, brethren, note those who cause divisions and offenses, contrary to the doctrine which you learned, and avoid them.*

18 *For those who are such do not serve our Lord Jesus Christ, but their own belly, and by smooth words and flattering speech deceive the hearts of the simple.*

19 *For your obedience has become known to all. Therefore I am glad on your behalf; but I want you to be wise in what is good, and simple concerning evil.*

20 *And the God of peace will crush Satan under your feet shortly. The grace of our Lord Jesus Christ [be] with you. Amen.*

21 *Timothy, my fellow worker, and Lucius, Jason, and Sosipater, my countrymen, greet you.*

22 *I, Tertius, who wrote [this] epistle, greet you in the Lord.*

23 *Gaius, my host and [the host] of the whole church, greets you. Erastus, the treasurer of the city, greets you, and Quartus, a brother.*

24 *The grace of our Lord Jesus Christ [be] with you all. Amen.*

25 *Now to Him who is able to establish you according to my gospel and the preaching of Jesus Christ, according to the revelation of the mystery kept secret since the world began*

26 *but now made manifest, and by the prophetic Scriptures made known to all nations, according*

holy kiss (v. 16)—a show of affection for friends, on the forehead, cheek, or beard; carried over from Jewish tradition

serve . . . their own belly (v. 18)—false teachers driven by self-interest and self-gratification

the whole church (v. 23)—the congregation that met in Gaius's house

establish (v. 25)—to make firm, stable, fast; that is, being rooted in the truth of the gospel

to the commandment of the everlasting God, for
obedience to the faith—

²⁷ to God, alone wise, [be] glory through Jesus
Christ forever. Amen.

Understanding the Text

2) What ministry plans and dreams did Paul have as he awaited his release?

_____

_____

_____

> **Underline the numerous verbs and descriptive phrases
> Paul uses in 15:14–33 to refer to his labor for the Lord.**

3) What insights into the work and structure of the first-century church can
we glean from Paul's personal greetings in chapter 16?

_____

_____

_____

_____

> **Circle the names Paul mentions in chapter 16.**

4) In the middle of this warm benediction, Paul includes a brief, but grave,
warning against harmful teachings and practices. What specific instruction
does he give?

_____

_____

_____

_____

Cross-Reference

Consider Luke's record of Paul's difficult, but much-longed for arrival at Rome in Acts 28:11–16.

11 *After three months we sailed in an Alexandrian ship whose figurehead was the Twin Brothers, which had wintered at the island.*

12 *And landing at Syracuse, we stayed three days.*

13 *From there we circled round and reached Rhegium. And after one day the south wind blew; and the next day we came to Puteoli,*

14 *where we found brethren, and were invited to stay with them seven days. And so we went toward Rome.*

15 *And from there, when the brethren heard about us, they came to meet us as far as Appii Forum and Three Inns. When Paul saw them, he thanked God and took courage.*

16 *Now when we came to Rome, the centurion delivered the prisoners to the captain of the guard; but Paul was permitted to dwell by himself with the soldier who guarded him.*

Exploring the Meaning

5) How does this passage illustrate the mutual affection between Paul and his brothers and sisters in Christ at Rome?

_____

_____

_____

_____

6) Read 2 Timothy 1:16–18. For what is Onesiphorus remembered?

_____

_____

_____

_____

7) Read 2 Corinthians 8:2–4. What instructions or principles for giving does Paul share with the church at Corinth?

_____

_____

_____

Summing Up . . .

"The people God uses to accomplish His will are His instruments, and no Christian should take personal credit for what God does through him. No brush takes credit for a masterpiece it was used to paint. No violin takes credit for the beautiful music the musician makes with it. Neither should a Christian deny or belittle what God has done through him because that would be to deny and belittle God's own work."—*John MacArthur*

Reflecting on the Text

8) A modern-day Christian says, "Why should I get involved in ministry? That's what we pay the church staff for! And all these appeals for money— I'd like to help, but I've got bills to pay. Besides, the church seems to get by nicely whether I give or not."

How might the believers listed in chapter 16 (or the Apostle Paul) respond?

_____

_____

_____

9) Imagine yourself sitting among the believers at Rome as Paul's letter was being read for the first time. How might the words of this final chapter have affected you and your brothers and sisters? Why?

_____

_____

_____

10) Now that you've completed this study of Romans, write a short doxology, expressing your praise to God for all He has done in your life through Christ:

_____

_____

_____

_____

Recording Your Thoughts

_____

_____

_____

_____

_____

_____

_____

_____

_____

_____

_____

For further study, see the following passages:

Acts 2:19
1 Corinthians 1:27–29
2 Corinthians 4:5–6
Philippians 2:17
Colossians 2:2–3
Revelation 22:7, 12, 20

Acts 16:7
1 Corinthians 3:6
Galatians 2:9–10
Philippians 3:18–19
1 Timothy 4:6

Acts 18:1–3
1 Corinthians 14:3
Ephesians 3:3–9, 20–21
Philippians 4:22
Hebrews 13:20